# THE
# MARRIAGE
# MECHANIC

## A DYNAMIC APPROACH TO A SUCCESSFUL RELATIONSHIP

## ANDREW V. PUSEY

LocalExperts™
People Building Our Community

LOCAL EXPERTS PUBLISHING

1st edition 2023

**Published By:**

Local Experts Publishing

224 – 1978 Yonge St, Toronto | Ontario | Canada | M4S 1Z7

647.507.8250 | LocalExpertsGroup@gmail.com

**Author's Contact:**

To book the author to speak at your next event or to order bulk copies of this book, please, use the information below:

631.258.9729 | andrewpusey711@yahoo.com

# ENDORSEMENTS & TESTIMONIALS

"Wishing you all the best and success with the launching of your new book on marriage. Remember, in marriage, love is in the sacrifice."

Bishop Noel Jones
Pastor – City of Refuge Church
Gardena, California

"Andrew has shown himself to be honorable, steadfast, and obedient to all that God has called him to accomplish. He is a strong leader, a good listener, and has been the picture of a devoted and loving husband."

Wife - Odetta Alves-Pusey

"If this uniquely and deeply inspired book does not lead a person to want an intimate relationship with Jesus and their spouse, nothing will. I want those I love the most to read this."

Apostle Dr. Delroy Smith
Author, Releasing The Greater in you

""The Marriage Mechanic" is a thoughtful and insightful exploration of the intricacies and dynamics of marriage. The Author's compassionate approach shines through as he delves into the fundamental aspects of a successful marriage. From communication and trust to navigating challenges and fostering growth, the book offers practical wisdom and invaluable advice to couples at any stage of their journey. Its thought-provoking content, Godly perspective, and practical advice make it an invaluable resource for individuals seeking to build and nurture strong and fulfilling marriages."

James A Douglas II
Family Life counselor, Marriage Life Director, Musical Director

"Bishop Andrew Pusey's inspiration to write "The Marriage Mechanic" comes at a time of significant challenges for marriage both for Christians and non-Christians. We live in an age where we face some of the most daunting challenges regarding ethical and moral issues. According to Barner Research, divorce is widespread. Their study discovered that one-third, thirty-three percent, of married couples, have experienced at least one divorce. Evangelical and non-evangelical born-again Christians' divorce figure is statistically identical to that of non-born-again adults, thirty-two percent versus thirty-three percent, respectively. In the face of this increasingly adversarial culture for marriage Bishop Pusey's book "Marriage Mechanic" takes its reader on a journey to a powerful, spirit-filled joyful life of experiencing marriage the way God intended it to be."

Bishop Steve Smith
Administrative Bishop – Church of God
New York State

"After all these many years of knowing and listening to Bishop Andrew Pusey, I have always been impressed by his assertive and impactful sermons. I am often in awe of his strong prophetic and evangelistic anointing. He has a way of leaving you wanting more of his powerful messages. Fortunately, he is delivering more words of enlightenment with this, his second book. Bishop Pusey's take on the sacred commitment of marriage will challenge you, as well as give you food for thought. It is not surprising to me that he would be inspired to write such a book - The Marriage Mechanics - since he took his time in finding his bride. I am certain that following the guidance in this book will enrich your life greatly and strengthen your marriage or give you the tools to build a strong marriage when you choose to pursue it. Read this book - you won't regret it!"

Avelyn Smith
Educator. Deaconess at True Life Church of God
& National Sales Director Emeritus with Mary Kay Cosmetics.

"Bishop Andrew Pusey is a very noble man. A man who has a passion for the word of God. A man who follows instructions. A man whose character and moral standards are very high. A man who you can depend upon, a man who you can rest assured for good advice. A man who is capable of taking care of his family, a man who shoulders his responsibility. A man who loves the Lord. I have known him for over seven years, and I can rest assured that whatever responsibility, whatever you place in the hands of Bishop Pusey, he is prepared and capable of handling it and will deliver it to the best of his ability. He has a lot of self-reliance and self-confidence. Most assuredly, I can tell you, he is my son-in-law;

he's married to my daughter. He has the values and qualities that a father-in-law would expect from a son-in-law. Thank you."

Mr. Philbert Alves (Father-in-law)

Mahaicony, Guyana

"Twenty years ago, Bishop Andrew Pusey came into our lives when I moved to New York to serve as State Youth Director for the NYCOG. Not only is he a colleague but a friend. Bishop Pusey is a man of integrity and impeccable character. His ministry, which spans over two decades, gives him a well-balanced perspective on life and ministry as a whole. I'm so impressed with this new book he has written. I recommend it to married couples as a great resource to build a successful marriage. It is also a great tool for couples' ministries."

Bishop Andrew Binda

Field Director of Asia/ Pacific - Church of God World

Missions

"Bishop and Prophet Andrew Pusey, is a man of high integrity and faith. For years I have known Bishop. He has always placed priority on marriage and family life. The words, guidance, and council from this book come from a life of integrity and consistency. I highly recommend them."

Bishop Joseph Inniss

Pastor - World Vision NT Church of God

George Town, Guyana

"Bishop Andrew Pusey has earned the respect of the church community of which he is a part, as well as leaders and business associates in the corporate world. He is excited about his second book, which speaks profoundly about marriage and relationships. I, therefore, recommend this book to youths and adults alike, married and prospective marriage couples. I am sure that you will enjoy Bishop Pusey's perspectives."

Bishop Raymond L. Rose
District Overseer, New York – Church of God - Melville

"Bishop Andrew Pusey, I have known you for approximately 14 years. From the time of our meeting, you have been a faithful, honorable, trustworthy, confidential friend. You love the Lord with every fiber of your being, and you are always seeking to uplift someone in their spirit by encouraging them to walk with the Lord. You are not judgmental and not always quick to condemn, but always seek to encourage and support for the best end result. You are loved and respected by your peers. You love your wife, mother, and siblings and take the matters that concern them seriously. You are responsible and dependable and always a man of your word. I pray that the blessing and anointing of God will continue to overflow and overtake you with every step that you take in your life, whether personally or in Ministry. God bless you always."

Min. Andrea Stultz
Realtor - Keller Williams, Jamaica

"Andrew Pusey is a passionate servant of the Lord who is always looking for opportunities to use his God-given gifts and calling to minister to the needs of people. His burning desire to make a difference in the lives of others and to play his part in extending the kingdom of God is part of what drives him to address this very important subject of marriage. Andrew has strong convictions regarding the sacredness of marriage, and he seeks to practice the same in his daily life. The Marriage Mechanic reflects his views on the subject."

Dr. Hixford Allen
Senior Pastor: Bronxwood International Church of God


"On The Marriage Mechanic. In the beginning, God instituted marriage. Marriages are very important. It is a covenant that God has established, called a blood covenant. Marriage can only end by death. Nothing else can come into a marriage to separate this union. So what God has joined together, let no man put asunder; God established marriage. Marriage is a love covenant, and love covers a multitude of sins. God keeps you as you embark upon this book of marriage that the great man of God has put together. May it help you, may it strengthen you, and may it protect you, in Jesus' Name."

Apostle L. Haynes
Senior Pastor - Tabernacle of Victory


"Marriage is a beautiful and awesome institution. My account of marriage is one that consists of constant work. "I am the true vine, and my Father is the husbandman. Every branch in me that beareth not fruit he taketh away: and every branch that beareth fruit, he purgeth it, that it may bring forth more fruit" John 15: 1-2. This captures the duty of the Husbandman. In order for the marriage to be fruitful, there has to be an accountability of duty and a commitment to work at bearing fruits. There is a beauty in serving and how wonderful that service is when it starts with our wives and husband. Stay blessed."

Mr. & Mrs. David & D. Hutchinson
Canada

"There is something about the power of God in someone's life. When the power of God is in someone's life, there is nothing too hard for that person. Bishop Andrew Pusey is such a person. God has worked through him in my life and in the life of others I know. I am sure any project he works on will have the power of God in it."

Rev. Andre Allen
Fresh Start Ministries

"Marriage Mechanic is a powerful exposition on how a successful relationship should work. Bishop Pusey captures some of the fundamental concepts. This book is a must-read."

Bishop Ransford Jones
Canada

"I've known Bishop Andrew V. Pusey for over 20 years. He's a man of purpose. He knows what he wants and is determined to get it, which has resulted in numerous observed successes. He's a man of faith who never quits or gives up."

Bishop Richard Queensborough
Pastor - True Life Church,
New York

"I have had the opportunity to observe Bishop Andrew Pusey

from the days that I taught him in Sunday School, in his early years, to his adult years as a minister of the gospel, husband, and entrepreneur. Bishop Pusey's journey was marked by many of the challenges of being a young Christian in Jamaica. The strict life of piety and godliness, that was required by parents and church leaders, was always challenged by the lure of a culture that glamorized promiscuous behavior and quick wealth through crime, violence and other illicit means. These overwhelming pressures did not deter Bishop Pusey in his quest for a deeper understanding of the mysteries of God. With this deeply passionate curiosity, he garnered time-honored truths from careful study of the Word of God and also from his many life experiences. Bishop Pusey has surmounted the obstacles he encountered and presents to us insights that are essential for his relationship with God as well as the human relationships we share with each other."

Rev. Christopher Hutchinson J.P.
Sr Pastor – Christian Fellowship – World Outreach Inc. (Jamaica)

"Andrew Pusey is an associate Real Estate Broker and has been associated with me, Richard Parisi, at Century 21 Parisi Realty for over 15 years. In that time, I have had the pleasure of seeing him solve dozens of housing problems for many families with honesty, integrity, and genuine care. His patience and persistence has made him a success as a Realtor. And more importantly, as a man of faith in Word and deed, yes, he touched the lives of many. Those fortunate to come in contact with him will know this as well as I do."

Richard Parisi
President - General Manager - Century 21 Parisi Realty

"You're a man of great exemplary integrity, leader, exemplary prophet, bishop, evangelist, teacher....you'll be pastoring one of these days, all these things. You are an exemplary husband and also exemplary friend and I'm so proud of you. Keep up the good work that you're doing and keep on letting your light shine. Everyone who comes in contact with you, have seen your life and that's the light of Jesus. I am praying for you, God Bless you."

Dr . Michael Hunter,
Pastor, Eagle Rest Church

*To my wife, Odetta Alves-Pusey, a Proverbs 31 woman with keen insight into ethics and etiquette. You often demonstrate wisdom, dignity, and excellence in all things. You are loyal and continue to stand by my side through thick and thin. I am pleased and grateful to you for that, with utmost love, appreciation, and sincerity. Our future is blessed with many things which God has promised. May our posterity reap the benefits of this book's wisdom.*

*'Shalom'*

ANDREW V. PUSEY

**"Marriage is honorable in all, and the bed undefiled: But whoremongers and adulterers God will judge."**

**Hebrews 13:4**

# CONTENTS

# ACKNOWLEDGEMENTS

In my second book, "*The Marriage Mechanic*," I couldn't have harnessed so much drive to write this book had it not been for the help of the Holy Spirit's wisdom and the various help in my formative years.

I want to acknowledge my wife Odetta, my parents, my family, my friends, my in-laws, my church family, and the Christian community for being honorable to us.

Especially, I again delightfully acknowledge my pastor, the late Bis. Dr. JA. Douglas and his wife, Rev. Dr. Roslyn Douglas, who were my spiritual parents in the gospel.

I want to thank the Holy Spirit for inspiring and leading me to write this book.

I want to thank my New York State Bishop, Bis. Steve Smith. He has been another tower of prayer and assurance over the years.

I also would like to acknowledge our friends and our colleagues Bishop Andrew Binda, Bishop Noel Jones, Bishop Queensborough, Bishop Rose, Dr. Allen, Bishop Inniss, Bishop R. Jones, Pastor Hutchinson, Rev. A Allen, Rev. Jimmy Douglas, Mr. Alves, Mr. Parisi, Rev. Stultz, Dr. Hunter, Deaconess A. Smith, Mr. & Mrs. D Hutchinson, Apostle Haynes, and Apostle Dr. Delroy Smith for their comments, endorsements, and testimonials in this book "The Marriage Mechanic." I appreciate your candor and generosity.

Last but not least, I acknowledge and thank the publishing company Local Expert Group and Dr. Raymond Harlall, for their undivided attention, expertise, and commitment to making this book a success. I do recommend you to the next writer.

# INTRODUCTION

*"²¹ And the Lord God caused a deep sleep to fall upon Adam, and he slept: and he took one of his ribs, and closed up the flesh instead thereof; ²² And the rib, which the Lord God had taken from man, made he a woman, and brought her unto the man. ²³ And the rib, which the LORD God had taken from man, made he a woman, and brought her unto the man."*

*Genesis 2:21-23*

This book, "*The Marriage Mechanic*", is about marriage and the dynamics of marriage when God formed man.

It is like a mechanical introduction to the life of a married person and will help readers understand the very beginning and nature of marriage. When we think of marriage, we think of the first institution God created and laid out for man.

God made the first example when he made man out of the dust and formed woman out of the man. Furthermore, he created her out of the rib of Adam. The Bible says that God called a woman out of man. He said, this is bone of my bones and flesh of my flesh. She shall be called woman; because you came out of the man.

So you know, your wife is a part of you. She came out to you, out of your side. She has your spirit; God has purposes for her in your life for His kingdom. Do not allow anything to sidetrack you from marriage.

*The Marriage Mechanic* is a metaphor like a mechanical tune-up. Just as a mechanical tune-up involves fine-tuning and adjusting the parts of a machine to make it function better, "The Marriage Mechanics" focuses on fine-tuning and adjusting aspects of a marriage to improve it. Just like a vehicle or equipment needing to change oil, change breaks, or reset some things, sometimes, we're going for miles, and we need a service. We need to be reset. Sometimes, we need to grease our shocks. We need to get rid of the terrain wear and tear; we need to be prepared for marriage.

And in marriage, when circumstances and situations do arrive, we know that we are prepared and ready to fight the battle that is before us. A marriage is a lot of work. Similar to how you wouldn't run your car for so many miles without a tune-up, you just can't run the marriage with so many miles like that. We do need a good tune-up.

## How This Book Is Structured

In this book, "*The Marriage Mechanic*," I speak about the different vicissitudes of marriage, and I give you tips.

In Chapter one, I give you a brief history of myself and how I met my wife. In chapter two, I speak about what marriage is and marriage as the first institution. In Chapter three, I address the principles of marriage, and in chapter four, I talk about the system of marriage to help lay the foundational understanding of marriage. In Chapter 5, we dive into the tune-up and explore marriage romance tips and advice we need to "tune up."

In Chapter 6, I bring your awareness to the Jezebel spirit, which could be a spirit that is at work behind the scenes. And finally, in Chapters 7 & 8, I touch on fathers in marriage and the favor of God that comes with marriage. Proverbs 18:22 says "he that finds a wife, finds a good thing, and obtains favor of the Lord."

In this book, you'll be able to grasp and understand the different dynamics that come with marriage. You'll be able to comprehend and navigate through the unique challenges, ultimately empowering you to withstand the test of time.

I want you to be successful in your marriage. And I wrote this book because I want your marriage to work and run smoothly, like a new Ferrari.

# Chapter 1

## Brief History and How I Met My Wife

I was born and raised in the Parish of St. Andrew, Jamaica. I attended the Stella Maris Preparatory School. It was a Catholic school, and during those days, we were trained to be disciplined as youngsters. I did track and field for a few years. I ran for my school, went to the Miami Classic, and represented my school growing up. I did very well in school. I attended extra classes with my peers and received first place in my class several times. I was academically successful throughout preparatory school right up until the final exam called "Common Entrance" at the time. My performance got me through to St. George's College in Kingston, Jamaica, my heart's desire. St. George's College was one of the top schools back then, and it is still one of the top schools in Jamaica, at the time of writing this book. I was so glad that I was able to attend that school. I attended St. George's College in 1992 and successfully graduated in 1997 with CXC subjects in Business.

It was during my high school years that I got saved. I gave my heart to Jesus and got saved on July 22nd, 1993. However, navigating through school and my teenage years proved to be quite challenging, despite having found my faith. It took me a while before I decided to get baptized. The following year, on January 2nd, 1994, I got baptized. Having found my faith, I joined the youth choir, and I was able to sing for the glory of God. While being part of the choir, my passion for Ministry came to me. I was able to minister in the streets in the volatile areas of Grants Pen and other areas in and around Kingston like Shortwood, Barbican, White Hall, and Waka Pen. Typically, these areas were impoverished regions where violence was prevalent due to widespread poverty. With an evangelism team spearheaded by my mother, I witnessed many gunmen give their hearts to Jesus Christ throughout the time.

It was great growing up. I had a lot of activities while in school and attended church every day. Yes, I attended church daily, Monday, Tuesday, Wednesday, Thursday, Friday, Saturday, and Sunday. I walked miles from home to church every day for choir practice, youth fellowship, Bible study, and other sessions I attended with the church. During this time, they were also constructing the church building. We had the opportunity to contribute to the construction of the building, aiding in creating that remarkable structure. Throughout my youth, there was always a balance between school, church, and personal growth and development.

## The Migration Catalyst

On nine different occasions, gunmen held me up, and God saved me. How? Why did He save me? Those experiences made me say a bold prayer one day, "Lord, if You let me go to the United States, I will serve You. I will do whatever You say and become a preacher." The same week, I learned that my father was filing for my siblings and me to receive US residency. Before this prayer, I had no idea this was in the making. I woke up one morning from a dream where I vividly remember seeing a yellow paper. When we checked the mail, there was the yellow paper; the mail that had come was my approved US residency paperwork. I interpreted that as God's confirmation to come to the United States. Talk about answered prayer!

In preparation to leave, I got the blessing and prayers from my Pastor in Jamaica, Bishop Douglas, and Reverend Douglas, and I was sent off with tributes from the youth choir and the youth fellowship.

I had such a grand time while migrating to the United States. I came here with one suitcase, I trusted God, and I went into the Ministry. God allowed me to graduate from Bible School, and I was ordained as a minister with the Church of God and grew through the ranks.

## Meeting Odetta

Through my mission in the Ministry, I got the opportunity to go to Guyana. The calling to carry out this mission felt very deep, and I thought it was meant to be for me. Little did I know that

God was using it as a channel. This mission led me to meet my wife, Odetta.

A friend of mine who was close to her grandmother thought it was a good idea for her granddaughter, Odetta, and I to meet. To myself, I thought, "I've never really had an interest in pursuing someone in Guyana." But my friend insisted that I try to make a friend. So I did; I tried. For the first time, on May 5th, 2016, we spoke. After that connection, I planned on waiting for the weekend to call or text her, but I don't know what pushed me to text her that same night. She responded immediately, and from there on, we had a good camaraderie, and she took an interest in my Jamaican accent.

Given my age and success in Ministry, she was curious about my relationship status. She wondered, "Why are you not married yet?" I told her not many women would take on the burden of the Ministry; that places a challenge on settling down into a relationship.

We had great conversations in the following days. So much so that one Saturday, I had an appointment to do my real estate prospecting. I got dressed and spoke with her on Skype, which was intended to be for a little while. I ended up talking to her for five hours and forgot all about my real estate appointment. It was such a nice time. We frequently spoke for hours on end on the phone, had great conversations, and built a great friendship.

That summer, just in time for the 4th of July, she could finally visit the United States, and I met her face-to-face for the first time.

When I saw her, I had no doubt, I had the greatest feeling inside me; this will be my wife. I felt it deep in my soul. Peace washed over me. I picked her up at the airport and took her to my brother's house, where she stayed with him and his wife. They also grew a liking for her.

## Building Our Friendship

During her visit, we went on dates. I took a two-hour long drive to Montauk on Long Island. It was such a peaceful and tranquil setting where we just rested and relaxed. We had a good time.

I gave her a heart-shaped diamond promise ring. My former bishop's wife told me to always try to give a promise ring and make some kind of commitment because I was excited when I met her. When I gave it to her, she looked at me, and she cried; she felt fearful. I assured her this was not an engagement; it was just a promise to say that I was committed to you and this relationship. She took it, and we hugged; I felt such a warmth within my soul and within my heart. We had several excursions.

Thereafter, she met other members of my family, and we continued building our friendship and bonding. Funny story, at this point, though her grandmother was the mutual contact between my friend and Odetta, I never met her grandmother first. I met my wife first. She returned to Guyana, and we both looked forward to the next time we would see each other again.

We decided to go to Jamaica together and had a wonderful time. We went to Negril; we enjoyed ourselves at a beach, Dunn's River Falls, and built that love and trust in our bond. While in Jamaica, I took her to my former pastor, Bishop Douglas, and his wife. He is from the old school and drilled her with questions wanting to see her surety. She was a bit nervous there, but she came through okay.

They left us with two tips:

1. Never tell family anything bad about your partner because they will not forget it even when you forgive him or her.

2. Always remember the value you first saw in each other when you just met.

We went back to the United States and spent some time together there; we went to Florida, visited SeaWorld and Disney World, and continued building that friendship. She eventually went back home to Guyana and her family. We communicated through Skype, and it was at this time that I virtually met her father through Skype. "You are a lucky man," he said to me.

I went to visit her in December of that year, and I met her family. I traveled with her to Wakenaam to meet her grandparents in person for the first time, and we had such a wonderful time with her grandparents. While there, we took a boat across the Essequibo River to Wakenaam Island, and we drove back to Georgetown, where I was able to meet her mom for the very first time and her brother Glendon, with whom I had great fellowship.

## About Odetta

Odetta is a very professional, confident, competent, driven Financial Analyst and Project Management Professional with over six years of managerial experience in the public sector. She is an enthusiastic and dedicated professional with high integrity, a strong work ethic, and very impactable interpersonal skills in the field of Project Management.

Odetta grew up in Mahaicony, Guyana. She attended the Mahaicony Secondary School, then she went on to Presidents College and was successful in many CXC subjects in Business. She then attended the University of Guyana, graduating with a Bachelor's in Economics. She then furthered her studies and completed her MBA at the University of the West Indies.

When I met Odetta, she was working with the Ministry of Finance. Though busy, she sacrificed some time when I visited. We spent time connecting, we had great times, and we built over the years. We had our different vicissitudes of the relationship but were able to stand.

Initially, her folks never understood me. I was Jamaican, and they had their own culture and beliefs. She made that clear. But it was okay because that was a part of the dynamics. When someone is from a different culture, you'll be skeptical towards them. But I stood and maintained who I am, maintained my character, my integrity. Over the years, people began to respect me.

## The Proposal

I remember it like it was yesterday. I went to Guyana, to the "Sea Wall" behind the Pegasus Hotel, and planned to propose to my wife; she took the proposal lightly. I made a more official proposal when she came to the United States up East in Mattituck by Love Lane; this time, she accepted. So here she was, a very private person, and I was able to make a more private proposal as we had to navigate the different cultures.

Following the proposal, we took our time to plan out our future together. We took our time to get to know each other, and as all couples do, we had our ups and downs. I had actually hoped that she would stay in the United States until we got married; however, it did not work out that way, and she went back to Guyana. This all happened in 2017.

In early 2018, I visited Guyana to preach at her father's birthday celebration. A few months later, her grandmother passed away. Unfortunately, Odetta was in Grenada and was transitioning to China in a few weeks through New York. I was unable to go to her grandmother's funeral in Guyana, but I was able to meet up with her in New York and comforted her during her loss before she went on to China for two weeks. She was sorrowful but remained strong.

When she returned to the United States, we sat down and discussed getting married and wedding plans. My initial request was for us to get married in Guyana. And her preference was to get married in New York. When she eventually returned to Guyana, she told her family about our decision, and they were excited for us. They were also excited about the wedding; however, due to financial constraints and lack of travel documents, most of her family would have been unable to travel to New York for the wedding; Guyana was a more convenient option.

## The Wedding

I contacted the Bishop of my church in New York, Bishop Steve Smith, and he agreed to officiate the wedding. October 22nd, 2018, at 5:00 PM, we made it official in Farmingdale, New York.

Her grandmother's best friend graced us with her presence at the wedding along with my family, and we had a dinner celebration afterward. We sang together and had a good time. It felt very refreshing to know that we were finally married. We embraced the feeling of two coming together as one.

## At Last... Then COVID

At last, Odetta's US residency application came through, and she could finally and officially come to live with me in the United States. Shortly after she landed and started to settle in, the pandemic hit, and for almost a year, she was home without work; it was a very frustrating time for us. But all things worked together for good; we went through the different vicissitudes of life and could stand amidst it.

My wife stood with me, and I stood with her irrespective of the storms of life, regardless of how we felt sometimes. She was able to be there for me as my wife, and I was there for her as her husband. God worked it out with us throughout the difficult times and challenges. We stood because I believe in the scripture, which says, "He who has begun a good work in you will perform it until the day of Jesus Christ." When God starts something, He finishes what He starts. When God opens the door, no man can close it. And if God gives you your wife, nobody can take her from you because it's the hand of God that puts you together. When God puts you together, no man can tear you apart or pull you down.

## Prayers for Unity & Strength

I've had friends who stood with me over the years that I want to acknowledge. Dr. Hunter and Bishop Green stood with me as friends. Many of my colleagues prayed with me and prayed for us. My former Pastor, Bishop Dr. James Augustus Douglas, and his wife, Rev. Dr. Douglas, would call and pray for us and for the strengthening of our souls. They prayed that God would keep us together and whom God has joined together let no man put asunder. They prayed that a threefold cord would never be broken and that God would bind us together with cords that cannot be broken. My Dad prayed for us, asking that the Lord God join us with chains that cannot be broken; we will remain together in unity.

Sometimes you'll become weary, tired, and worn. But I want to tell you, you can stay together if God is in the midst of it, and you shall be blessed. You'll be delivered. You'll be set free. You'll stand up amidst the storms of life. You'll stand up amidst all the challenges, trials, and tribulations. God will be there for you and hold you up and keep you from falling.

He says, "Now unto Him, that He is able to keep you from falling and to present you faultless before the presence of His glory with exceeding joy onto God our Savior be glory, majesty, and power. Both now and forevermore." He'll hold you up amidst whatever enemies you may face. He'll turn it around, and He'll make it good. He'll open up the windows of heaven and pour a blessing upon you that no man can stop. No man can obliterate. No man can deny it. Because when God gives you access, nothing can stop or thwart the plan of God in your life. Your plans are His plan in your life. So you have to stay focused in spite of some tribulations that you may face.

## Resources and Wisdom

Over the years, I've read many books on marriage, including The Five Love Languages, Naked Marriage, and The Speed Of Favor, among many others. These resources built me as a person so that I'm not torn down easily in my marriage. You need books, other resources, and others' wisdom. Sometimes in order to sustain your life, you need counsel from trustworthy sources. You need the Bible; you need the Word of God. You need prayer. You need unity and fellowship in order to stand in your marriage because sometimes the storm clouds do rise. But when God is in it, you will win it. You can stand the test of time knowing that He has begun a good work within you; He will perform it until the day of Jesus Christ.

I'm so thrilled, so happy to be married to Odetta Alves-Pusey. I am so delighted to have her as my wife. And I appreciate her every day of my life. I accept her. I know that it's the will of God. Our union is divine. God chose me as a Minister, and I chose her as my wife, and I thank God for putting us in each other's path and allowing us to come together. And I know that there is a great divine purpose that God has in store for us, and it's going to be accomplished in unity. It's going to be accomplished together. Because when two of us agree to work together, it shall bear bountiful fruit. It shall be done by the will of our Father who is in heaven. God is in our midst, and we will succeed.

# CHAPTER 2

## THE FIRST INSTITUTION

Marriage was the first institution in the Bible. Jesus' first miracle was at a marriage in Cana of Galilee. We need to understand the importance of marriage. God does not make mistakes when He works and performs. If we reflect on the fact that in Genesis, the first institution He created was marriage, and the first miracle was at a wedding, we see God prioritizes marriage and it's sanctity.

We need to understand that the revelation of God is spiritual. When God moves, He's strategic; He's spiritual. He sees the end from the beginning. The revelation of God is not physical. The revelation of God is not material. The revelation of God is not mystical. God's revelation is spiritual, indicating a spiritual connection and experience between you and God.

When God looked at Adam in the Garden of Eden, He told Adam that it is not good for man to be alone. But how could Adam be alone if God was there? God's relationship with us is not physical, and man needs someone for him apart from God.

We often say that the Lord is our husband, but from this physical point of view, God can never be your husband. In the creation of Eve, Adam's wife, God put his nurse's garment in his hospital under the sky or the tent of the sky, then the same God became an anesthesiologist and put him to sleep, put him to bed in the hospital. The same God became a bone surgeon and cut the man open with a surgical instrument. The same God became a human constructor and built a woman out of the bones of man, became the woman's father, brought her to the man, became the preacher, and said, who gives this woman to be the bride of this man? Isn't that God? God is a powerful God.

## Blood and Wine

Wine represents the blood we need to speak the blood of Jesus over our marriages. You see, marriage is very important and a very crucial aspect in our lives. That is why the first thing the enemy attacks is the home, because he knows that is where the structure stands. Since the world stands in the family, Satan doesn't like to see people together. He'll try everything in the book to tear you apart, but if God be for us, who can be against us?

It is funny to see how Jesus turned water into wine as His first miracle. Many of us condemn wine and hold negative opinions about various aspects related to wine. I don't know the theology behind it, but it's funny to see how Jesus turned water into wine when He was present at a wedding.

Wine is a byproduct of grapes. It is formed out of the crushing of the grapes. When we are crushed in our spirit, something comes out. Something must come out of you when the enemy pushes you, ties you up, and presses on you. I don't know what Adam was going through in the Garden of Eden. He was a lonely man. Occasionally, we find ourselves surrounded by a plethora of things. We have money with cars and animals and everything around us. We have the church community, but still, we find ourselves feeling lonely on the inside. Sometimes, that loneliness crushes us, and something comes out of us.

Wine represents the blood. I don't know what's been crushing you, tying you down, or holding you back, but something is coming out of your persecution. Something is coming out of your crushing. He told them to fill up the water pots. You have to give God something to work with. God will work with the little faith that you have. Give God something to work with. Give God something to move with, and God will work with it.

I've said to someone, your husband is not going to fall from the skies; your wife is not going to fall from the skies. You have to make your movements. He that finds a wife, finds a good thing and obtains favor from the Lord. God loves marriage; He loves unity. He loves to see couples together. I'm talking about the sanctity of marriage. The sanctity of a true marriage between a man and a woman. It's in crushing and oppressing that things come out. Things come out of people in the circumstances.

You never know somebody until you are in a circumstance with them, where conflict comes, and everything that's down on the deep recesses and caverns of his soul comes out. Everything they share with the entire world stems from the depths of their emotions, and that inner turmoil surfaces during arguments or moments of frustration. Pressure has a way of causing emotional outbursts. When a tire bursts out on the road, it is pressure causes that tire to burst. Sometimes when things are inside of you, they need to burst out of you. That's why we can't put new wine in old wineskin because it'll cause it to burst. You have to clean up your vessel and allow God to move through you, allow God to manifest through you. Do you know that we are the bride of Christ, and He is our groom? That's why God loves marriage because it's a symbol. It is a type of "Christ and the church".

Look it up in the scripture: Marriage represents Christ and the church, so **God respects and honors marriage and that makes a great difference in marriage. He respects marriage, which is why when it comes to marriage, you should not play in people's marriages. Keep out because that's something that God respects.**

## Water Pots and Vessels

St. John chapter 2 mentions water pots. Sometimes our vessels are drained and empty and need a refilling with wine, which is the spirit of God. The songwriter says, "...fill my cup, Lord. Fill it up. I lift it up, come and quench this thirsting of my soul." I thought about the woman at the well. She was at the well and at midday, and she was thirsty, and she needed some water to drink, and here came Jesus Christ, and He was able to tell her all that she'd been through. He could tell her how many marriages she had. Jesus Christ was able to give her water that would allow her never to thirst again. He was that living water that will cause you never to thirst again.

So Jesus had that conversation, and you know what? She thought He was an ordinary man that she could probably talk to and flirt with and get to become her husband. She never knew that this was a time of change in her life, a living water, a salvation experience. Sometimes you're thirsty, but your thirst indicates that there's a change that's about to come. There is a difference that's about to take place in your life, that God is about to turn your thirst into a river. The power out of your belly shall flow rivers of living water.

The Bible says, and be drunken not with wine as ye supposed, but be filled with the Spirit. Don't be drunk with the regular wine but be filled with the Holy Ghost, be filled with the pirit of the living God. Let God fill your vessel. Let God fill your marriage with joy and happiness.

The Bible says in Romans chapter 14 that the Kingdom of God is not meat and drink but righteousness, peace, and joy in the Holy Ghost. The Holy Ghost will give it joy. God will bring joy to your marriage. Happiness comes from the Holy Ghost. You see God, He covers and hovers over the affairs of men. The Holy Ghost will give you joy. If you need some joy in your life, the Holy Ghost will give you that joy, give you that happiness, give you that peace. Nehemiah says in chapter 8:10, neither be sorry for the joy of the Lord is your strength. If you're weak today, God's going to give you some joy. God's going to give you some happiness. He's going to give you some peace, and He's going to give you some love. He's going to operate on every platform in your marriage, every platform in your life, and every platform in your family; God will give you some support, and He will manifest joy.

## Drink Water From Your Own Cistern

"Drink water from your own cistern and running water from your own well."
Proverbs 5:15

Then the scripture says, in John 7:38, "...out of your belly (your innermost being) shall flow rivers of living water." I want to tell you that you can tap into what God is placed inside of your spirit. God has invested some great and powerful things inside of your soul, and you can tap into it through the Holy Spirit and receive what God has placed inside of you. The well is deep. It needs something to draw; the Holy Ghost will help with drawing out what is placed inside of you.

Proverbs 5:18-19 says, "[18]Let thy fountain be blessed: and rejoice with the wife of thy youth. [19]Let her be as the loving hind and pleasant roe; let her breasts satisfy thee at all times; and be thou ravished always with her love."

Proverbs 18:21-22 says, "[21]Death and life are in the power of the tongue: and they that love it shall eat the fruit thereof. [22]Whoso findeth a wife findeth a good thing, and obtaineth favor of the LORD." To receive favor from God, you have to be on a quest with God to get a wife. It's not she that finds a man. No, it's he who finds a wife. It is not that he finds a girlfriend. It is not that he found a sister in the church. But rather, he that finds a wife. In other words, you have to be of wife material for him to locate you. So he then finds a wife is a blessing. Let thy fountain be blessed and rejoice with the wife of thy youth.

You have to know how to believe in the sanctity of marriage and have respect for marriage. It's not going in and out of it. It's not bouncing here, there, and everywhere, and to each his own. And I say this not to speak based on a theological point of view but my own beliefs. You married her. That's it. Until death do us part. That was the vow you made to God. You said in sickness and health; for better or for worse, we make a mockery out of the thing many times. We make mistakes, we understand, but the truth will still be the truth. It says in sickness and in health. That's the vow. For better or for worse, that is the vow. Marriage still stands amidst the world's twisted views; two men can't produce. It's a man and a woman. Be fruitful and multiply and replenish. Even a plumber knows that; even an electrician knows that. Male and female. So we ought to keep it the way it should be and not twist it, nor turn it. It's what the word says, and if the word says it, it is forever settled in heaven. God's going to look at us one day and say to us, you did not run well. Who did this to you? You did not obey the truth, and His word is a truth.

## Forgiveness and Cleanliness

You know that unforgiveness can send you to hell. You ought to get rid of unforgiveness. We've got to have some love. Some prophecy in God's name, and cast out demons in His name, Jesus is going to say on that day, "depart from Me; I know you not." I don't want God to say that to me. I don't want anything to come between me and God on that day. Oh, we have to clean up our vessels. In order to get some clean water, we have to clean the vessel. Get the vessel clean and sanded. Get the vessel washed and purified. Are you washed in the blood of the lamb? Are you white as snow? Are you washed in the blood? Are you free from the burden of sin?

David said I'm going to bless the Lord at all times. His praises shall continually be in my mouth. No matter how your marriage is, no matter how your home is, you're going to bless God. We keep standing, no matter the twist and turns, try to keep the "church" as a pure garment. We keep her clean and spotless; keep it white. We keep it pure because we're the bride of Christ. No matter what's happening on the outside, keep your garment pure. The church is still secure, still steadfast. The church still moves on no matter what. The battle comes; no matter what may come, the church will be the church, unstoppable, unmovable, always

THE MARRIAGE MECHANIC    25

abounding in the work of the Lord. We know that your labor is not in vain in the Lord. You shall see a victory like never before. God's turning around. God is turning your circumstance around. Your circumstance will not define what God has purposed, because He's turning it around. He is giving you favor. I'm speaking grace over you. There's healing and deliverance. There is a breakthrough.

Ephesians 5:26 says that He might sanctify it and cleanse it with the washing of water by the word. God is coming for a glorious church. There were ten virgins, according to Matthew chapter 5, and it was a time where five were wise, and five were foolish, but they all had the same resources; they all had vessels, but they weren't prepared. So prepare your vessel and get ready for God. Don't be foolish but be wise. Allow God to breathe himself upon you. He has begun a good work in you, and I will perform it on the day of Jesus Christ. Be not weary in well doing, for you shall reap.

## Be Persistent and Steadfast

Don't allow circumstances or situations or that cunning devil, that subtle devil, to interfere with what God has purposed in your life. Stay the course. Remember the fire, the passion God has placed inside of you, and allow him to bring it to pass. You have to be persistent. You have to be steadfast in this. I don't know if your patience ran out. I don't know if your zero ran out. I don't know if your resources were depleted. I don't know what ran out in the middle of your wedding. The wine, the main thing that everybody comes for, ran out. I want to encourage you today that no matter what runs out when Jesus is there, he will turn it around.

Turn your water into wine. You see, water is a tasteless substance. It doesn't have any taste, so you are going to get them water at a wedding. They want wine, but sometimes we don't know what God is doing. We have to be obedient to the cause and call of God. We have to be obedient to what God is saying to the order and distinction of God. We have to be obedient to the purpose of God. Walk in line and do what He said, what Mary said. His mother said, whatever He said unto you, just do it; just be obedient to God. You're going to see your best days ahead of you. The governor of the feast said we have never had wine so good like this. You always put the best wine first, but at this feast, you save the best wine for last. It's a mystery, the last shall be first. Don't give up. The race is not finished, the task is not over, and God is not through. It is not a battle for the strong, but he that endures to the end.

Ecclesiastes 9:11 says "[11]that the race is not to the swift, nor the battle to the strong, neither yet bread to the wise, nor yet riches to men of understanding, nor yet favor to men of skill; but time and chance happeneth to them all." Wait upon the Lord. Your change is coming. You may not know how. He can turn your circumstances around. He can turn what's twisted and make it straight. Your crooked path shall be made straight. I don't know what the situation is, but God is going to put some wine into your water.

Think of the words "bitter" and "better". These two different words came into my spirit, bitter and better. I realize that Jesus is the "E" in bitter, which makes it better. So when you remove the "I", yourself, out of bitter and put Him, which is "E", into your bitterness, you become better. I don't know what's happening in your life, but God says He's turning your "I". He's getting you out of the way and putting Himself, which is the "E", in your bitter, and it's going to get better.

God is about to give you some new wine. After all the crushing that you have been through, your wine is going to be sweet. When you drink that marriage wine, you are going to be drunk, not as you suppose, but you're going to be filled with the Holy Ghost. The spirit of God is going to take full control.

# CHAPTER 3

## THE PRINCIPLES OF MARRIAGE

Marriage is an institution. It's the first institution created by God. God is the founder of marriage. Therefore it is the oldest institution in the world. God created men in His image, male and female, created He them, and said unto them, be fruitful and multiply and increase in numbers. Replenish the earth, the imperatives of marriage. Marriage is the only means for a proper sexual relationship. Marriage is honorable in all, according to Hebrews chapter 13, and the bed is kept pure for God. For God will judge the adulterers and the sexually immoral. So marriage is honorable; the bed is undefiled or, in other words, kept pure. For God will judge the adulterers and the sexually impure. 1 Corinthians 7:9 says that if they cannot control themselves, they should marry, for it's better to marry than burn with passion.

Marriage provides a sense of belonging, one to the other. Marriage gives you a sense of care, protection, and belonging. According to Genesis 2:18, "18And the LORD God said, It is not good that the man should be alone; I will make him a help meet for him."

Also, 1 Corinthians 7:2 says, "²Nevertheless, to avoid fornica-tion, let every man have his own wife, and let every woman have her own husband." The wife's body does not belong to her alone but also to her husband. In the same way, the husband's body does not belong to him alone but also to his wife.

All well-established organizations and institutions are governed by principles. In fact, they cannot stand without principles. Therefore, since marriage is the bedrock of all institutions, it is paramount that the principles are observed.

In John 2 Jesus Christ set his approval on marriage by attending a wedding. While He was here in the world, Jesus and the disciples were also invited to the Cana of Galilee's wedding. According to Matthew chapter 5, Jesus also referred to the first marriage in the Garden of Eden and set out the principles in the beginning; the creator made male and female and said, for this reason, a man shall leave his father and mother and be united with his wife, and the two shall become one flesh. So they are no longer two but one. Therefore, what God has joined together, let no man separate.

## Biblical Principles For Wives

According to Ephesians 5:22, wives submit yourselves to their own husbands as to the Lord. Verse 24 goes on to say, wives submit to their own husbands in everything, and verse 33 says wives must respect their husbands.

Colossians 3:18 says, "wives submit yourselves, submit to your husband as it is fitting in the Lord." Titus 2:4 says to train the younger woman to love their husbands and children, to be self-controlled and pure, to be busy at home, to be kind, and to be subject to their husbands. I Peter 3:1 says, wives, in the same way, be submissive to your husbands.

When they see the purity and reverence of your lives, they shall be won by a chaste conversation. Beauty should not come from outward adornings. Instead, it should be that of the inner self, the unfading beauty of a gentle and quiet spirit, which is in the sight of God.

## Biblical Principles For Husbands

Ephesians 5:25 says, husbands love your wives; wives respect your husbands. Husbands should love their wives, and according to Ephesians 5:28, husbands ought to love their wives as their own bodies. Ephesians 5:28 says, "each of you must love his wife as he loves himself." He that loves his wife loves himself.

In Colossians 3:19, He says, "husbands love your wives and be not harsh with them." 1 Peter 3:7, "husbands, in the same, will be considerate as you live with your wives and treat them with respect as a weaker partner."

The reality of marriage, the marriage vow is a sole agreement that should not be broken. Therefore, you should be prepared to keep the agreement. By all means, after the marriage vow is taken, you both will become one, one life, one love, one purpose, one pursuit, and one purse; in other words, your finances are also one.

## Requirements of a Successful Marriage

* Both parents and friends should be considered outsiders to the intimate relationship.

* All personal secrets must be uncovered before the vow is taken.

* Quality of tolerance must be cultivated. The truth is, abnormalities and flaws may be discovered or occur after the vows are taken.

* Adjustments of lifestyles are imperative for the development of the marriage union.

* It is very important that you pray together, plan together, and play together.

* There must be equal sharing with each other.

* When a child or children should come along, you should share equally; equally sharing among all family members is the only ground for unity, peace, and progress.

1 Corinthians 13 says it requires a quality of true love for a successful marriage. It reads, "Love is patient, love is kind. It does not envy, it does not boast, it is not proud. It does not dishonor others, it is not self-seeking, it is not easily angered, it keeps no record of wrongs. Love does not delight in evil but rejoices with the truth. It always protects, always trusts, always hopes, always perseveres. Love never fails."

True love will help you make the necessary adjustments for a happy and successful married life. True love is essential for the sense of a happy and successful life. Now it says to have a love and a happy marriage or how to have a love and a happy marriage these days, perhaps the greatest source of happiness in life is a contented marriage with the right person, a peaceful home, and lovely children to bless it. It is your wish. If you are already married, you can have a happy marriage. Love and a happy marriage are exactly what God wants you to have. In the very first chapter of the Bible, God tells you that men and women were made for each other. It is not good that the man should be alone. I'll send a helpmeet for him. Those are God's own words. You see, God made men and women for each other's joy and love.

## God's Timing & Love

Would you like to be in love to get married? God has planted your yearning for love within your heart, and He will satisfy it. God wants you to know there is nothing so beautiful as meeting the one meant for you. And God wants lovemaking to be very happy. He does not want you to be old when you are young. He wants you to be happy—wholesome love between men and women.

You will be lucky if love comes to you out of comradeship and friendship. Many times, just one encounter may decide your destiny, even though you may not see the other for weeks, months, or even years. Some deep instincts give a man the power to see the honesty and sincerity in the art of a plain girlfriend. So do not be disappointed if you do not feel as beautiful as others. We should be thankful to our Father that love can come to all love entering in, not by the doors, but by the heart. Love comes to the plain just as to the pretty. Love comes to the poor as well as the rich. Love comes to the older as well as the younger. Love has no age or cage.

Sometimes you are lonely and say, how can I find love and make myself charming, handsome, and ready for love? How can I marry?

The time is in God's hands, but the way is in yours.

Many men wait patiently while love stirs in their hearts. Many women wait and wonder and hope before love is awakened in the heart of a man. The real way to charm love is through the heart, and the way of the heart is to love. Yes, learn to love all persons and all things and be appreciative. The more people you love, the more radiant you'll become.

Love will turn to you as naturally as a flower turns to the sun. Attract love by usually liking the man or the woman who goes around saying; I don't like this kind of man. They pick flaws in everyone they meet and rarely find anyone they like, and in return, no one will like them. The key is "like" turns into "love". So we must like people, like them enough to go where they are. Go to church and church affairs. It may not happen by chance. You may meet someone in church work or church affairs. That same inspiration that connects your heart together will connect you to God. This is because of your union, your agreement in love. Just the power of love will transform you. You'll be a new person because love creates love and is very creative. It is a new person in you that your mate will see.

Try to associate yourself with different people. You cannot meet your mate if you stay home. You will meet your mate through exposure to friendship; you'll know deep down in your heart that he or she is the one when you meet them and know them, like the rising chord of a great organ. The course of love runs from companionship and courtship to the sacrament of marriage, and with marriage comes a new life.

Love and marriage are through God. To break into anger and to interfere, to insist on finding details of marriage affairs accomplishes nothing. The uplifted heart, the open Bible, the bent knee, the prayer-hearing, and the prayer entering God; these alone can bring peace and harmony to your home. With God, you can love. Love suffers long and is kind. Love is not easily provoked. Love thinks no evil. Love bears all things and believes all things, hopes all things, and endures all things.

## God In Your Marriage

Growing in your unfolding brings you to a very close relationship with God, who is the root of life. We forgive the erring ones and love them in spite of their sins. When you trust in God, your love and marriage problems begin to change. When you position yourself for a happy marriage and a happy home, a new peace from God transcends your soul. The way of love and marriage is the way of God, the love, the family, the husband, and our wife. God gave you this opportunity, which He gave you to carry out His plan for you.

A family that prays together stays together. God wants us to build up our love connection. He wants to build up our spiritual relationship. He wants to build up our romance, emotional attachments, creativity, and financial stability.

Be sensitive to the needs of your wife, physical attractiveness, and sexual intimacy. God wants to build you up; things don't just happen overnight; it takes time. For example, emotional attachments take time. And when the emotional attachment is present, sexual intimacy will flow and increase passionately.

## Tips On Building An Emotional Attachment

- Try to call or text.

- Leave your wife a love note.

- Do not misinterpret rejection.

- Touch, caress, and cuddle your wife.

- Be affectionate to her.

- Be thoughtful many times thinking about each other.

- Reciprocate your love and your emotional needs.

- Try to be affectionate.

- Seize every opportunity, every moment to be there for your wife or your husband.

- Be compassionate and show genuine care for your spouse.

You have to try and build a marriage in every aspect. Marriage is very important. It's something that you can be able to look at for years to come. It is like an investment.

- Be sensitive to your wife.

- Give each other that space and that solitude to do your

individual things. Build up yourselves together, individually and collectively as a unit.

- Try different ways and means to build yourselves up together.

- Listen before you make assumptions about your praise, and don't criticize too much.

- Be constructive in your criticism of your bride and your spouse.

- You can disagree, but don't be disrespectful, especially before your children.

- You want to try to apologize when you're wrong and forgive. No one to be silent and one to speak.

- Don't be angry. As the scripture says, don't let the sun go down on your wrath.

- Be sensitive to each other's needs and desires.

**These are paramount to your intimacy:**

- Know each other's moods and feelings.

- Help to diffuse anger and misunderstanding. This will enhance intimacy.

- Know when she is going through a certain rough time of

the month, you have to be very sensitive. Time is crucial.

- When making important decisions, make sure you notify your partner when making decisions.

- Plan with your partner. Don't plan a major event in your life without your spouse. Always make your spouse know what you're doing.

- Be very clear and transparent with your spouse.

- You have to know what button to touch or what button not to touch. Be very sensitive.

There is a time and place for everything. When to touch, when to talk, when to play; you have to know those things.

- Acknowledging each other's presence is very important.

- Be very, very open and receptive to your spouse.

- You have to tithe together, budget together, spend properly, and build savings together. Build investments together. Build retirement together. According to Ecclesiastes 10:19, "...but money answereth all things." Try to budget as much as possible together.

## Sex, Intimacy, and Romance


When you meet your spouse's intimacy, you, your love, and your sex life begin to become fuller. Love will get stronger. You'll be content; you'll be harmonious; you'll be happy. Love will be lasting. It'll be satisfying. There'll be great fulfillment in the marriage.

When you don't meet the spouse's intimacy, there's a withdrawal syndrome. Sex begins to dwindle. Lack of cooperation, feelings of misery, and anger can arise. Different things may happen, and you don't want that silent treatment or cold shoulder. We don't want any infidelity; we don't want anything to interfere with our marriage. So try and build up those areas that are important.

Be creative. Stretch your imagination. Do things out of the ordinary. Surprise your wife. Change up some things. Go on dates spontaneously. Go for a huge, exotic, small, or mini vacation. Go shopping together. Buy your wife nice gifts. Change the atmosphere, change things around sometimes. Help her with your house, the house chores and et cetera. Be surprising. Be there for your spouse. Try to build up your spouse in every aspect.

Build up your romance: romance is key. Cuddle and caress. Be happy to see each other. Be there for your wife to show chivalry. Build up the passion. Build up the Romance. Build up the flame. Be kind to each other. Make a home a safe haven of comfort, love, and compassion. The bedroom is the most romantic place. Keep that sacred. Come with yourselves to be romantic. Men, put on your cologne, dress neat, and smell fresh. Women, dress sexy and smell fresh and sweet. Have nice dinners together. Walk and hold hands. Watch movies together, shower together. Be creative and romantic. Yes, make your marriage effective.

Plan rendezvous. Go on dates. Sometimes romance is setting the stage. It's committing yourself. You have to be very committed to being romantic. Romance is the glow of intimacy. Romance keeps the heat in your marriage.

Work out together. Get in shape together. Walk. Go to a gym together. Get fit and versatile with each other. You know, you'll appreciate and reap the benefit of physical attractiveness. Try to maintain a healthy lifestyle and eat well. Rest well, have a proper diet, exercise, and visit the doctors frequently. Less sugar intake because sugar can work against your sexual performance. Keep strong, healthy, fit, and relaxed. A spouse will help you to be very performing and satisfied. Physical attractiveness is a plus for intimacy. Every spouse wants to know that their mate is good in health and shape and gives maximum performance.

Build up your sexual intimacy. Sex is God's design. It's the design, pleasure and protection, and preservation of marriage. Sex is multidimensional and warm. It is a gift that you must use to maximize your marriage to accomplish intimacy and fulfillment.

Talk to each other. Love each other. Express feelings and desires to each other. Make sex a priority, a high priority in the marriage. Be stimulated. Keep off of Viagra; instead, exercise, and have a clear mind that helps your sex life. Make it meaningful, exciting, and unforgettable. Do it as often as you can. Create the mood and the atmosphere. Make your spouse feel desired.

Men, be hygienic, be fresh and ready. Impediments to sexual intimacy are a lot of sickness. Inflexible sickness, erectile dysfunction, premature ejaculation, pornography and abuse in the past, selfishness, and infidelity. Be loyal to your wife or your husband. Be hopeful and sensitive to the atmosphere: be creative, spontaneous, and flexible. It will help you to reach the zenith or the top in sexual fulfillment.

Have fun. Do not use sex to manipulate your spouse, but let it be a tool of intimacy. Sex is God's design to preserve, protect, to build. This is a gift that you must use to maximize the marriage. Accomplish great intimacy and sexual function. Sex is key. Make sex a priority, and change the atmosphere. Be very romantic with your spouse. Being romantic is key and very, very much important.

## Communication & Love

Communication is key. Watch out for non-verbal communication. Be a good listener. Poor communication is a disaster in marriage; "a soft answer turns away wrath or grievous words, stir anger." Use language, the love of languages. When you communicate with your spouse, be endearing. Show her love, say, honey. Say, "my love." Say, "babe," say, "dear." This can positively affect your marriage when you are endearing as much as possible. On the flip side, don't call your spouse's name out of anger: be enduring.

Men value honesty. A man is assured when he knows his wife is trustworthy, responsible, reliable, and honest. Communicate with him sincerely. Tell him how you feel; he's not a psychic. You have to communicate with your spouse in order for them to understand what you're thinking and feeling.

Men usually talk in general; women want to be specific. Be clear, open, and specific about what you're saying, so your spouse can easily understand. Communication is absolutely important to healthy, intimate marriage. Talk to each other romantically and sexually; it will enhance intimacy. Communication is key to understanding each other's needs, desires, and feelings. It is key to understanding what you're thinking or what you're aspiring to, what you're looking for. When an airplane is flying, they have to communicate with a tower to take off and land.

Connect with the agape love. That's the basis for love. Love each other genuinely and passionately. Intoxicate yourself with love. Connect yourself to the marriage. In other words, blend yourself into the marriage.

Marriage is honorable, and the bed is undefiled. Be kind. Be courteous. Just be patient with each other. Be affectionate. This will stimulate love and build up your desire for intimacy. Love is a foundation on which we establish and perpetuate. Build up our marriage desires. Each of us must feel genuine power, passion, love, and energy toward each other. Love one another deeply.

## Lack Of Intimacy

Many marriages suffer because of the lack of intimacy. It is a deep cry in the coverings of the soul. When a silent cry, folks need that kind of touch. Whatever kind of intimacy you have, they need to be shared, whether psychological, emotional, physical, sexual, or spiritual; a deep level of intimacy is needed. And there are steps to genuine lasting intimacy. If you apply them in your life, you reap dynamic benefits.

Many marriages will be better when intimacy is rekindled. Your intimacy is a deep personal connection between each other. It is that kind of warmth, love, affection, and deep feeling for your spouse. Women tend to define intimacy as verbal communication, while men define intimacy as a shared activity.

Everybody defines intimacy differently. Love without intimacy is immoral, according to one writer. People who have successfully built an intimate relationship know his power and comfort. So care and intimacy fills our hearts—a deep longing for closeness and affection. Intimacy in a relationship is the single most important thing that will cause you to enjoy, enhance, build, and embrace your marriage. So promote intimacy.

Another part of your marriage is spiritual connections. That's very important when you connect spiritually. The union between a man and woman is God's design and purpose for true intimacy to be expressed, revealed, and discovered. Marriage, covenant, and consummation are the deep and most performed ways for your intimacy. Your commitment to God and your spouse will enable you to fulfill the need for spiritual intimacy.

Pray for each other. Knowing and applying the principle of God's word will enable both of you to grow spiritually and intimately. Spiritual connection is a foundation on which we build our lives in intimacy. The oneness of the Holy Spirit will allow your intimacy to deepen and become saturated and merged. It will tie into your marriage's spiritual, emotional, and psychological factors. You want to build your intimacy. You want to build your marriage. You want to make your marriage work. You want your marriage to become that bedrock of success.

Seize that opportunity to build an emotional attachment to your spouse. Show genuine care for your spouse. Surprise each other. Help each other with house chores to change up sometimes; be spontaneous. There are many ways to build your marriage. When a man is diligent and intentionally makes his wife feel loved, like the queen she is, she'll reciprocate. She will deliberately honor him and respect him. Love her like a queen, and they said that she'd honor you like a king.

Show undivided attention to your woman. Women like to know that their husband has them as the center of his world. She appreciates, respects, and honors you when she knows you are considerate and compliments her. When you make her feel that way, it gives her a sense of security in marriage. It empowers her and makes her feel special. Your thoughtfulness and focus on her will allow confidence in her to begin to surface. This will help to foster confidence. It'll build a strong and secure marriage.

Intentional attention to your wife is an investment that will bring fruit benefits to your marriage, allowing you to be attentive to her. So show affection, show admiration, and appreciation, and try to articulate as much as possible with your spouse. I'm telling you, it's going to get there. It's going to get better and better and better. You know, you will develop a greater and very efficient marriage whenever you are connected with your spouse.

# CHAPTER 4

## THE SYSTEM OF MARRIAGE

*"²²Wives, submit yourselves unto your own husbands, as unto the Lord. ²³For the husband is the head of the wife, even as Christ is the head of the church: and he is the saviour of the body. ²⁴Therefore as the church is subject unto Christ, so let the wives be to their own husbands in every thing. ²⁵Husbands, love your wives, even as Christ also loved the church, and gave himself for it; ²⁶That he might sanctify and cleanse it with the washing of water by the word, ²⁷That he might present it to himself a glorious church, not having spot, or wrinkle, or any such thing; but that it should be holy and without blemish. ²⁸So ought men to love their wives as their own bodies. He that loveth his wife loveth himself. ²⁹For no man ever yet hated his own flesh; but nourisheth and cherisheth it, even as the Lord the church: ³⁰For we are members of his body, of his flesh, and of his bones. ³¹For this cause shall a man leave his father and mother, and shall be joined unto his wife, and they two shall be one flesh. ³²This is a great mystery: but I speak concerning Christ and the church. ³³Nevertheless let every one of you in particular so love his wife even as himself; and the wife see that she reverence her husband."*

*Ephesians 5:22-33*

*"And the Pharisees also, who were covetous, heard all these things:
and they derided him. [15]And he said unto them, Ye are they which
justify yourselves before men; but God knoweth your hearts: for that
which is highly esteemed among men is abomination in the sight of
God. [16]The law and the prophets were until John: since that time the
kingdom of God is preached, and every man presseth into it. [17]And
it is easier for heaven and earth to pass, than one tittle of the law
to fail. [18]Whosoever putteth away his wife, and marrieth another,
committeth adultery: and whosoever marrieth her that is put away
from her husband committeth adultery."*

*Luke 16:14-18*

## Marriage, Divorce, and Remarriage

The Christian marriage is made for forever. That scripture is
not easy to comprehend, ascertain or understand.

It says in Romans 7:1-3, "[1]Know ye not, brethren, (for I speak
to them that know the law,) how that the law hath dominion over
a man as long as he liveth? [2]For the woman which hath a husband
is bound by the law to her husband so long as he liveth; but if the
husband be dead, she is loosed from the law of her husband. [3]So
then if, while her husband liveth, she be married to another man,
she shall be called an adulteress: but if her husband be dead, she
is free from that law; so that she is no adulteress, though she be
married to another man."

Divorce and remarriage are very difficult, and there is a pressing
need for some clear teaching on the subject. We must be loyal to

scripture and not be carried away by the opinion of men. When a divorce has taken place, it is often impossible to undo the damage that has been done. It usually results in such a tangle of complicated situations that no human being can easily unravel. I speak with sympathy toward those who are entangled with marital disasters, struggles, and issues. But **I'm speaking specifically towards helping to prevent the tragedy of divorce from happening in the lives of folks.** The knowledge that the Bible doesn't permit divorce and remarriage is a powerful fact in helping people to determine that they're going to make their marriages work.

Divorce and remarriage are certainly not new subjects. First, divorce is not a problem nowadays. Moses had to contend with it. The question was brought to Jesus over 2000 years ago. They asked if it is lawful for a man to put away his wife. And Jesus gave the answer. He says that because of the hardness of your heart, that's why God permitted divorce. But from the beginning, it was not so.

John the Baptist lost his head because of divorce and remarriage, a challenge that he brought to Herod. Herod, who was responsible for John's execution, had imprisoned him because of his disapproval of Herod's relationship with his brother's wife. John confronted Herod about the woman, who happened to be Herod's brother Philip's wife, saying that their union was unlawful. He had told King Herod that the woman he married was not really his wife but that she was still the wife of Philip, her first husband. This enraged the woman. That's why she asked for the head of John the Baptist on Herod's birthday, and the king was sorry nevertheless for the oath's sake and those who sat with him at a meal. He commanded it to be given to her.

Divorce is evil, and separation and divorce have broken thousands of American homes. In 1887 there was rarely any such thing as divorce in the entire United States of America. But divorce has rapidly increased in our country. Approximately one out of every three marriages ends in divorce. There was a time when divorce carried a stigma and shame, but it no longer does. A grade school teacher asked one of our pupils to give his father's name. They replied, "Which one, teacher? I've got three fathers." The divorce law in some states is so loose and so full of loopholes that marriage often becomes a little more than a 30-day free trial. One writer says in some cases today, "the wedding cake lasts longer than the marriage itself."

## The Causes of Divorce and Remarriage

### Hasty Marriages

One of the causes is related to hasty marriages, that is, when folks marry too soon without knowing the person. You should have some insight and knowledge about the person you're getting married to before making this lifelong commitment. Only a miracle can sometimes prevent the tragedy in homes when people marry after they have known each other for only a few weeks; it takes more in-depth knowledge of someone to marry. Too many couples marry first and then get acquainted. We have many arranged marriages where this occurs in many instances, but sometimes things are beyond your control, and we do understand. But hasty marriages do cause a lot of instability in the structure of the marriage.

## Believers and Unbelievers

Marriage between believers and unbelievers often creates problems in homes because they are unequally yoked. We should be yoked with Christ, and many times, one is pulling one way and the other another way; one is trying to pray to Jesus. One is trying to pray to Krishna or other gods. Paul said not to be unequally yoked together with unbelievers for what fellowship has righteousness with unrighteousness and what communion has light with darkness, and what temple of God has to do with idols. Idols mix the things of God, of righteousness, with the unrighteous things, and that causes many marriages to be depleted.

## Prayerless Marriages

A prayerless marriage is also a factor related to divorce and remarriage. In each marriage, a couple should begin a family altar at the very beginning of the married life. If a young couple prays and asks God to lead them in their own married life and will keep the family altar going down through the years, there wouldn't be any divorce courts in all of the land to put their marriage on the rocks.

There is much truth to the slogan, "A marriage that prays together stays together."

## Hardness Of Heart and Adultery

What does the Bible say about divorce and remarriage? We must forget our sympathies at this point and what others say and what we have read in books and listened to. We must seek God's book and discover what it says. The vow says, "until death do us part."

Ecclesiastes 5:4-6 says, "[4]When thou vowest a vow unto God, defer not to pay it; for he hath no pleasure in fools: pay that which thou hast vowed. [5]Better is it that thou shouldest not vow, than that thou shouldest vow and not pay. [6]Suffer not thy mouth to cause thy flesh to sin; neither say thou before the angel, that it was an error: wherefore should God be angry at thy voice, and destroy the work of thine hands?"

While it is best not to separate, if a couple divorces, they are not free to remarry that union; then, it can only be dissolved, according to the scriptures. It says in 1 Corinthians 7, but if she departs, let her remain unmarried or be reconciled with her husband. I really believe that the channel should be left open so that the relationship can be restored in response to the partner's repentance, restitution, and restoration.

Divorce is not mentioned in the Bible until 2,500 years after the first marriage. It is true that God permitted divorce to the hardness of hearts, but from the beginning, it was not so. But Matthew 5:32 says, "But I say unto you, That whosoever shall put away his wife, saving for the cause of fornication, causeth her to commit adultery: and whosoever shall marry her that is divorced committeth adultery."

Here are a few more scriptures from God's Word on the subject:

Mark 10: 5 says, "[5]And Jesus answered and said unto them, For the hardness of your heart he wrote you this precept. [6]But from the beginning of the creation God made them male and female. 7For this cause shall a man leave his father and mother, and cleave to his wife; [8]And they twain shall be one flesh: so then they are no more twain, but one flesh. [9]**What therefore God hath joined together, let not man put asunder.** [10]And in the house his disciples asked him again of the same matter. [11]And he saith unto them, Whosoever shall put away his wife, and marry another, committeth adultery against her. [12]And if a woman shall put away her husband, and be married to another, she committeth adultery."

Romans 7:1-2 says, "[1]Know ye not, brethren, (for I speak to them that know the law,) how that the law hath dominion over a man as long as he liveth? [2]For the woman which hath a husband is bound by the law to her husband so long as he liveth; but if the husband be dead, she is loosed from the law of her husband."

1 Corinthians 7:39. "The wife is bound by the law as long as her husband liveth; but if her husband be dead, she is at liberty to be married to whom she will; only in the Lord."

## God's View Of Divorce

God is not a fan of divorce. There are a number of scriptures that speak to this kind of situation. The scripture commands in Romans 12:8 to live peaceably with all men. If I get a divorce from my wife, I am not doing all the possible things to live at peace with her. I'm doing all I can to live peaceably without her, but not with her. Divorce also violates the command to forgive until 70 times seven, every divorce, no matter what, demonstrates an unforgiving spirit.

Everybody cannot receive the same because you have people who are beaten or abused by their partner to the point of their lives being threatened. That's a different story altogether, in my opinion. Divorce violates the plan to be faithful for better or for worse until death does us part. Divorce violates a topic in the Bible concerning going to the courts of the law. In 1 Corinthians 6, divorce violates a command in the Bible to be separate from the world. One who seeks divorce is following the example of Hollywood and not the law of God. The old tenor of the Bible is against divorce, and that's where it stands. There are different kinds of circumstances that people go through, and I understand, but the scripture still stands against divorce.

The Lord forgives the sin of divorce and remarriage just the same as he's willing to forgive any other sin. But remember, God expressed the sin to be discontinued. When a drunkard gets right with God, God expects him to quit his drinking and give up his bottle. So sometimes, some situations require us to make a rightful choice that's between God and us to work out our own salvation with fear and trembling. I said this within context, not to be judgmental in any way. Still, I want to explain the gravity of marriage and how serious marriage is that we do not take the institution for granted and do as we please in a way that opposes the scriptures. We don't want to walk contrary to the dictates of God and to scripture; we want to do things in the way that God is pleased and the way God gets the glory, the praise, and the honor.

We don't want to live our lives as covenant breakers and walk outside of scripture, and live ungodly. We just want to do the things that are pleasing to God in our lifestyle, in our mannerisms, and in our way. I believe that as Christians, we should live to please God and serve him with all of our hearts and mind, body, and soul. So as Christians, we should not allow this world to captivate us and to follow the dictates of the world and allow ourselves to be ostracized by the rules and the government of this world and for us to negate and deny God's precepts in his word. This is Jesus who said it. He says that if you marry somebody that's divorced, you commit adultery. He said that, it wasn't any other scriptures' opinion. So as long as you understand the base and the truth and the life of God, then you will not be tossed to and fro and put into a situation where we have to negate or cause our vows to be relinquished of not understanding the whole aspect of marriage and God. We don't want those things to interfere with God's plan for our lives because God says, I wish above all things that you will prosper and be in health even as your soul prospers. And when

God says that he wants you to apply it to your life, he wants you to let that become a structured area where you can walk in that joy and happiness.

Many times we make mistakes when young, and I understand that. But no, these passages are here for us to grasp the details and the gravity of marriage so that we don't enter into it and jump out. If we don't know what we are doing, we'll have to have to sit back and make a full decision about where God is taking us. And as long as God is in it, you will win it. You know, you don't have to question, you don't have to doubt, you don't have to wonder about that.

## Marital Success

If God is inside of your marriage, you are going to succeed in your marriage. You're going to prosper in your very marriage. Trust me, if God be for you, who can be against you? So you must allow God to have his preeminence and his way in your life, marriage, and home. Allow God to take complete control of everything, and it'll work out. God doesn't want to bind you and put you in bondage. He wants you to live freely in Him and to serve Him freely in the full and free salvation. And this chapter here is to give you that heads up and that understanding of what marriage truly is and how serious it is.

Marriage is connected to your eternal destiny. I wouldn't want to make the wrong decision at this time, totally regret it, and become rejected on the day of judgment because we never walked in honesty, truth, and love. We have to try our best as believers to allow the truth of God to be a part of our walk and our whole dialogue with scriptures so that we can live as believers in oneness and total connection with God. His truth still stands no matter how far we go, how high we climb; the truth of the scriptures remains steadfast. It's a cannon, the word of God that is quick and powerful and sharper than any sword. Nothing can come and dissect the word itself; it dissects everything it comes in contact with.

So as believers, we want to make sure that we make our calling and election sure. We will not fall by the wayside, and we will not allow the dictates of this world to govern our lives and cause our defeat in the kingdom. God wants us to be successful. God wants us to have marriages that are succeeding and prospering and not being defeated by the onslaught of the enemy. Satan comes to kill, steal and destroy. But Jesus said, "I've come that you might have life and that you may have it more abundantly." God wants you to have an abundant life.

As believers, we should understand that abundant life is essential for the believer. It's a whole holistic lifestyle. It's a full gamut of the kingdom of God. It's a full detail of what the plan of God is for life. Because God said, I wish above all things that you may prosper and be in health even as your soul prospers. He wants you to succeed just as though your spirit is succeeding. God wants you to become very successful in all your endeavors.

3 John 2 – Body, Soul, Spirit. The body is world conscious, the soul is self conscious, and the spirit is God conscious.

## A Traditional Marriage Vow

"I, ___, take thee, ___, to be my wedded wife/husband, to have and to hold from this day forward, for better, for worse, for richer, for poorer, in sickness and in health, to love and to cherish, till death do us part."

# CHAPTER 5

## MARRIAGE, ROMANCE TIPS & ADVICE

Here are some tips here on how to keep your marriage spiced up.

- You have to fight for your marriage.

- Wear something your spouse loves, share furniture, sit on his or her lap, and make a point to eat dinner together most days of the week.

- Never let your spouse feel like they come second place to your career or any other thing.

- Talk about your dreams and aspirations together.

- Be supportive of each other and dream big together.

- Maintain a united front as your motto, meaning me and you against the world.

- Speak well of your spouse, us against the world in every format and in every way.

- Make each other breakfast in bed.

- Do chores for her.

- Get a couple's massage or host your own privately.

- Dance together to soft music, and exercise together.

- Take bike riding together.

- Do hiking together.

- Choose not to be annoyed by your spouse's irritating behavior or disappointment.

- Thank your spouse often, even for a minor reason or gesture.

- Lay in bed together, and stare into each other's eyes without talking.

- Learn something new together. Take an art class or a cooking lesson.

- Leave a sweet comment on Facebook on the wall of your

spouse.

- Support each other's goals.

- Bring her flowers, gifts, nothing too expensive.

- Tell her she's pretty, especially when she does not feel so, and laugh together.

- Guard your marriage.

- Look out for the best interests of your spouse as often as possible.

- When you're together, take a break from the phones and technology.

- Forgive quickly.

- Be honest and find tangible ways to serve your mate without complaining every day, and argue fairly.

- Avoid words like "you always..." and "you never."

- Take one day a month to make your spouse your total focus.

- Compliment each other.

- Sometimes you leave work on time and come home early.

- Engage every day in meaningful conversation as much as possible.

- Women hang pictures of both of you around the house.

- Make their favorite dessert.

- Make sex a priority.

- Spend time apart occasionally.

- Learn to enjoy something he loves.

- Surprise your spouse.

- Meet him at the door.

- Text each other from across the room sometimes, like kids.

- Set reminders on your phone to remember him or her throughout the week.

- Call him right now and tell him you appreciate him.

- Go away together at least once a year.

- Renew your vows privately with whispers and memories.

- Sleep in his or her t-shirts.

- Read a marriage devotional together.

- Praise your spouse to other people.

- Wear T-shirts that tell the world you love your spouse.

- Revitalize romances with intimate dates.

- Buy him gifts he will love.

- Listen to music; share ear earbuds.

- Go to bed at the same time.

- Hide notes for each other.

- Go on dates regularly; have date nights regularly.

- Read scripture together.

- Always pray together.

- Always reach across from the front of your car seat when you drive and hold hands and even for a few moments.

- Tell her "you're the best"; call her from work.

- Often say, "I've been thinking of how great it is to have you in my life. Thanks for all that you are as a woman and all that you do for me and our family."

- Give her a pair of tickets to a theater show.

- Go an entire day without criticizing anything about her.

- Hugs and kisses every morning before you leave the house.

- Get to know her friends.

- Brag about her.

- Pray for her each morning.

There are so many things that you can do for your spouse. These are what I received as marriage advice.

- Never consider divorce as an option. God says, don't keep scores.

- Forgive quickly; function like two wings and the same bird.

- Find marriage mentors who are further along than your marriage.

- When choosing between saying nothing or something mean, say nothing every time.

- Don't assume you know what your spouse is thinking or feeling. Ask them. Your spouse doesn't always need your advice; sometimes a listening ear and a hug will go far away.

- Go to a good church together.

- Always wear your wedding ring. The ring symbolizes your union.

- Never talk badly about your spouse to other people or vent about them online.

- Be your spouse's biggest encourager, not their biggest critic.

- Embody a marriage that makes your kids excited to be married someday.

- Be patient with each other.

- Your spouse is always more important than your schedule.

Love is a commitment. It's not a feeling.

- Forgive instantly to promote healing.

- When trust is broken, be quick to say, I was wrong. I'm sorry. Please forgive me.

- Always answer the phone when your spouse is calling.

- Keep the phone off when you're spending time together.

- Surround yourselves with friends who will strengthen your marriage.

- Make laughter a part of your marriage.

- You are partners in everything. You'll win together, and you'll lose together. A strong marriage rarely has two strong people at the same time.

- Prioritize a bedroom. It takes more than sex to build a marriage, but it's nearly possible to build one without it.

- Marriage is not 50-50. It's 100% from both of you. Give your best to each other, not your leftovers.

- Learn from others.

- Don't put your marriage on hold while raising your kids or being a caregiver.

- Never keep secrets from each other.

- Never lie to each other.

- Be patient with each other.

- Communicate your frustration, and don't nag your spouse.

- You ought to maintain high standards in your marriage.

- Offer to work together.

- Find something to praise

- Build up your marriage in every area as much as possible because that's key.

Your marriage is where you're going to have the greatest core. Your marriage can either break you, or it can make you. Make sure you are steadfast in marriage because if somebody's not steadfast in his marriage, then everything is off. Learn how to be steadfast in your marriage and build it up.

## Romance Tips

Here are some romantic things that you could do together.

- Take a stroll around the block together.

- Give each other a back rub.

- Sit in front of the fireplace and talk.

- Write a poem for your spouse.

- Go the extra mile to please your mate.

- When you are the one who is correct during a discussion, give your spouse a kiss. Focus on your love rather than who is right.

- Tell your spouse; I'm glad I married you.

- Fulfill one of your spouse's fantasies.

- Hug your spouse from behind and give a kiss on the back of the neck.

- Create your own special holiday.

- Do something your spouse loves to do even though it doesn't interest you personally.

- While driving, pull over for a scenic site.

- Get out of the car to enjoy God's creation.

- Mail your spouse's love letters instead of spontaneously leaving them in the house.

- Spend the entire day together away from the house.

- Give your mate a foot massage.

- Develop a code word for sex to use when you are part of a crowd.

- Set up a surprise, manicure, or spa appointment.

- Read together and for one another.

- Plant a tree together in honor of your marriage.

- Bring home flowers.

- Surprise your wife when busy by saying, what can I do to help?

- Count the stars together, which are innumerable.

- Whisper something romantic to your spouse in a crowd.

- Have a candlelight picnic in the backyard.

- Write out 50 reasons you're glad to be married to your spouse.

- Place a rose on their pillow.

- Hide small gifts that your spouse will find throughout the week.

- Sit and listen carefully to one another.

- Dance in your candle-lit living room.

- Walk on the beach.

- Play a board game by the fireplace.

- Kiss in the rain.

- Join him unexpectedly in the shower.

- Use a tender touch as you pass one another around the house.

- Break away from the family long enough to share an intimate conversation.

- Kiss your spouse's fingers.

- Celebrate for no reason.

- Fill your bed with rose petals.

- Take a fun class together.

- Ride a bicycle Built for two.

- Tell your wife you'll take her anywhere she wants to go.

- Have a hot bubble bath ready for her when she comes home from a hard day.

It's fascinating how these small pieces of advice can play a significant role in building up your marriage. They have the power to make a tremendous difference, helping you create a fantastic and strong bond with your partner. Maintaining a stable and harmonious marriage is crucial, as it is vulnerable to attacks from the enemy. Satan's primary goal is to disrupt and destroy such unions. Since marriage forms the core of our lives, we must cherish it and allow God to work through it, using our relationship to bring glory to Him and further His kingdom. Being married and seeing the same person for 50 years or 30 years, for so long, it's not an easy thing to do.

I have some more tips for you.

- Tour a museum gallery together.

- Give your wife a bath and wash her hair.

- Give each other back rubs, write the love story of how you met, and get it printed out.

- Turn the lights down during dinner.

- Play music in the bedroom.

- Remember to look your spouse in the eyes while she tells you about her day.

- Make up names for each other.

- Ask for an isolated booth in a restaurant.

- Go horseback riding on the same horse.

- Watch the sun come up or go down together.

- Put on perfume or aftershave before going out.

- Take a train ride together.

- Read a romance novel together.

- Develop a weekly dining spot to meet for lunch.

- Put perfume on your bed sheets

- Write out 50 reasons you're glad to be married to your spouse.

- Sit and listen carefully to one another.

- Remember all you used to laugh at things you thought were funny.

- Reminisce through old photo albums together.

- Go away for a weekend.

- Leave teasing notes around the house to create an atmosphere of anticipation.

- Use a tender touch as you pass one another around the house.

- Wink and smile at your spouse from across the room.

- Hug for an extended period of time.

- Fall asleep holding each other.

- Call your husband during the day and remind him of your love for him.

- Ask your spouse, what can I do to make you happier?

- Try to go away for the weekend and spend only $20.

- Break your after-dinner routine and go sightseeing, reminisce about your first kiss and the first date.

## Spice it Up

These are some interesting things that we could do to spice up a romance because romance is very important in every marriage.

- Use chivalry.

- Open the car door for your wife or the house door.

- When you're there, compliment your wife and how she handled a difficult situation.

- Initiate daily prayers, make a commitment, and then begin to pray together every day.

- Begin by giving thanks to her and to your family.

- Then pray with her about her worries and challenges.

- Then ask her to pray for you about the challenges you're facing.

- Say, thank you after every meal she serves.

- Put the toilet seat down when you're finished and wash your hands.

- Write a short love letter. List several ways that she has blessed you this year.

- Fill her car with gas, and vacuum the mats.

- Wash your wife's car.

- Try making breakfast again.

- Call her, send her an email or text while she's in the mirror, come behind her, and gently kiss the back of her neck.

- Offer to brush her hair and compliment her.

- Tell her you are crazy about her.

- Call her from work.

- Let her choose where to dine.

- Wrap your hands around her after your morning alarm goes off, and tell her thanks for taking such good care of you.

- Each day, try to say, I love you in different ways.

- Tell her how much you enjoyed making love to her after the morning sex.

- If you have kids, tell your kids that you have got the best mom in the world. Isn't she great? I just love her so much. Help her Put the kids to bed at night.

- Tell your wife she's beautiful often.

- Don't ever stop giving her flowers.

- Don't always fix problems. Make her feel secure.

- Don't forget about foreplay; for some women mentally, foreplay is doing the dishes, taking out the trash, and bathing the kids.

- Encourage her dreams, pay tribute to her, and help her achieve those dreams.

- Ask her what her sexual needs are.

- Give her a list of reasons as to why you are so glad to marry her.

- Try to discuss any big changes or important decisions with your wife first.

- Relieve her occasionally if she is a stay-at-home mom, and take the kids away for the afternoon so she can enjoy herself.

There are so many ways of building that level of intimacy with your spouse, which is key in your marriage. You have to learn how to practice intimacy that will structure your marriage and cause your marriage to become even more passionate and intense in a better way. This will cause you to bond better.

Be sincere about what you do and say because that's the reason why she is with you. No woman is going to marry a man that she does not love because marriage is important to a woman, and if she doesn't love you, no true woman is going to marry you. Try to be very sensitive to your wife's needs.

## Questions For Your Spouse

Ask your spouse questions like...

- What are the top excuses you use to justify situations?

- What makes you feel loved?

- Ask her, what do you think I could do or you could do to come closer to God?

- What can you do to make someone feel better emotionally, spiritually?

- What are the best books to read?

- What makes you jealous?

- What makes you insecure?

- What are you most proud of in life?

- What does quality time mean for you?

- If you're rich, what will you do?

These questions are good conversation starters.

- What makes you happiest?

- What are your greatest strengths?

- What are your weaknesses?

- What are your top three priorities in life?

- What do you like to do when you're in your quiet time?

- What's the most romantic thing anyone has ever done for you?

- What scares you the most about marriage?

- How would your children describe you to others?

- What are your best and worst habits?

- What are the things that make you feel important?

- What's your biggest blessing and burden when it comes to your job?

- What do you think your love language is so you can work together in that area?

If you are unfamiliar with "The Five Love Languages" by Gary Chapman, the five love languages are physical touch, quality time, words of affirmation, gifts, and acts of service.

Sometimes one word itself can make a marriage even more cemented and concretized, greater. One word that the husband may have said may be able to stir a lot of good. Similarly, one word can stir a lot of bad in marriage. So just be careful. Be thoughtful about what you say to your spouse because whatever you say to your spouse can either cause good or bad.

## Sweet "Lyrics" For Your Spouse

Here are some powerful words you can say to get into your spouse's heart.

- Just one thought from you is enough to make me tremble.

- If a genie can grant me three wishes, I'd say your name three times.

- You know, I can say when the person you love loves you back, it's the greatest feeling in the world. Even science can't explain what I feel for you.

- I can't tell you what's so magnificent about love other than loving you.

- Your voice quiets my fears.

- Our love is the love they write books about.

- You can say even the bad days are brighter when you are around.

- Is it wrong for me to think about you every day, every other thought?

- As long as you are in my life, I believe I can do anything.

- I wish I hadn't met you yet so I can relive the day I first saw you.

- You can say you said I love you first, but I loved you long before I had the guts to tell you.

- I wonder how boring my life would be if we had not met.

- I can't help but smile when you are across from me.

- Thank you for staying in love with me.

- Your smile can make any flower bloom.

- If I could pick anyone on this planet, I'd pick you.

- I will never forget the day we fell in love.

- Never underestimate the power of true love for you. You changed my life. I don't want to go back to what it was.

- You're a song I keep wanting to hear.

- There was magic when I first saw you.

- Nothing comes close to the feeling of being loved by the person you love.

- It's crazy how I don't even notice the time when we're together.

- My name sounds so sweet coming from your lips.

- The most amazing thing in the world is falling in love with your best friend.

- No one person will ever love you like I do, not even you.

- When you smile at me, it makes my heart race and takes

my breath away.

- I used to think I was crazy for loving you until I realized I was just crazy in love with you.

- You and I were examples of two people becoming one.

- Let's love each other in a way that makes others better.

- I couldn't believe I survived all these years not knowing you.

- I have an all-consuming love for the woman you're becoming.

- I'll never get tired of holding your hand.

- Loving you was worth any price I had to pay.

- I never really knew what love was until you came into my life.

- Suddenly all of the love songs make sense.

- The only thing I regret about us is not meeting you sooner.

- There are more words to describe how I feel for you than there are stars in the skies.

- I would cross the ocean for you. I climb the mountain for you. I'll give my heart to you.

- You're an itch in my heart that I just can't scratch.

- I don't want any gifts except for your love and attention.

- Call me selfish, but I want you all to myself.

- All the superlatives are not enough to describe you.

- There's no sweeter sound than when you affectionately call my name.

- Let's make memories to tell our grandchildren someday.

- The only thing better than waking up next to you is laying with you.

- I've never liked anyone until I met you.

- You have a way of making even our normal days magical.

- You're mine, and you are enough.

- I can face all hardships in the world as long as you are with me.

- Don't forget that I'm here, and I will never let go.

- Let's make up for the days we hadn't met each other yet.

- I didn't know I needed you until I needed you. But I guess God already knew.

- I knew I had found the right woman because you made me forget all the wrong ones.

- People want success, popularity, and money, but all I want is you.

- We still have more songs to sing, more memories to make.

- I'll never regret the day I said I love you, but now I regret not being able to say it enough.

- I can't even remember what it's like not to love you.

- Months, years, or even centuries are not enough to show you how much I love you.

- I don't want any gifts except for your love and attention.

You have to build your love life. There are many things to talk about, many things to have conversations about in order to build your love life. Your love life is very important; it's a part of you as a man and as a woman.

## What is Love?

Love these days is defined as a profound, tender, passionate, affectionate feeling for another person. They say it is a feeling of warm fuzzy fuzziness. A Feeling of personal attachment or deep affection, passion, or desire. They say, in the worldly view, it is a strong preference, enthusiasm, or liking for anything.

The Holman dictionary describes love as an unselfish, loyal, and benevolent concern for the well-being of another. It says the word "charity" comes from the Latin "Caritas," which means dearness, affection, or high regard. Today, charity is seen as an act of benevolence. Other words for love are devotion to fidelity, involvement, fondness, piety, regard, respect, appreciation, enchantment, ardor, and support.

In today's world, love has become so meaningless. Love seems like it is just a ritual or vain repetition. Without God in your heart, you don't and will never know the meaning of true love. Love is that pillar that is rugged, grooved, and harnessed in God. Love is the pure foundation on which every other affection is built.

There are several forms of love. Here are a few:

1. Agape - which is the boundless love of God.

2. Storge - which is relationship compassion in marriage and family.

3. Philia - which is brotherly friendly love as in the city of Philadelphia

4. Eros - which is passionate love, erotic love between a male and a female.

5. Ludus - which is flirtatious, playful love,

6. Pragma - which is committed, lasting love.

7. Philautia - which is self-love.

We may have expressed love in acts of service towards one another, physical touch, quality time, receiving gifts, and words of affirmation.

## A Different Kind of Love

Every child of God has the capacity to love expressively. Love the expressive love. Love is God, and God is love; he that loves not knows not God because God is Love. So beloved, let's just love one another, for God is Love. Love is the oil that soothes the very friction in the engine. It is the hinges on which every door turns; it is the very itch in your heart that you just can't scratch.

You have to learn how to build and strengthen your marriage in every and any way because love is the key. Love is a cornerstone. Love is the structure that keeps you together. I pray that the hand of God will strengthen, encourage and give your marriage the courage to be taken to the next level because you'll stand every test of time, and you'll know that the Lord is with you. The Lord will keep your marriage. The Lord will strengthen your marriage.

God is the one who starts the good work in you and will perform it on the day of Jesus Christ. So God will strengthen and cause your marriage to be excel in the right format and the right category because, with God, all things are possible. If you trust and believe and love His Holy name.

# CHAPTER 6

## THE SPIRIT OF JEZEBEL

In this chapter, I am enlightened to talk about the spirit of Jezebel. We understand in Revelations 2:20-22 where it says, "²⁰Notwithstanding I have a few things against thee because thou sufferest that woman Jezebel, which calleth herself a prophetess, to teach and to seduce my servants to commit fornication, and to eat things sacrificed unto idols. ²¹And I gave her space to repent of her fornication, and she repented not. ²²Behold, I will cast her into a bed, and them that commit adultery with her into great tribulation, except they repent of their deeds."

We understand in the Old Testament that Jezebel was the wife of King Ahab. She was a domineering personality. She tried to control Israel through the strength of leadership within the confines of her husband's position. Jezebel was a sexually loose woman; it says that according to references, Jezebel taught false doctrine. The Bible does not mention Jezebel is a spirit, although it has plenty to say about Jezebel herself.

She was the great daughter of Ethbaal, King of Tyre and Sidon, and a priest of the cult of Baal, a cruel, senseless, revolting, false God whose worship involved sexual degradation and lewdness. Ahab, King of Israel, married Jezebel and led the nation into Baal worship. There are two incidents in the life of Jezebel that characterizes her and may define what is meant by the "Jezebel spirit." One trait is her obsessive passion for domineering and controlling others, especially in the spiritual realm.

Baal worship was closely associated with obsessive sensuality. Jezebel, as a daughter of the kingdom, was raised in an atmosphere where sex was a path to power and influence. The Jezebel spirit is born of witchcraft and rebellion. The demon is one of the most common spirits that is in operation today, both in our churches and in the world. We find that its power or influence makes it a powerful enemy to the body of Christ Jesus. She operated freely on sincere believers whose hearts are for Jesus individually and who have attained positions of power within the church.

## Characteristics of Jezebel

The spirit establishes strongholds primarily in women. Many men have been victimized by this spirit which functions to gain identity, glory, recognition, power, and satisfy the need for praise of men. The Jezebel spirit is a man hater and seeks to emasculate men, deprive them of their spirit or force, and divest them of their authority and power. It fosters distrust and hatred for men in general.

The Jezebel spirit is a constant agitation, terribly aggressive, very determined, callous, and controlling. The spirit is selfish, power-hungry, manipulative, unrepentant, deceitful, and overwhelmingly evil. The spirit can definitely be named a "Satan woman."

Jezebel operates by manipulating others and taking control of them in order to get things done to her desire. It is a Jezebel spirit that works in the heart and lives of people to control folks so that they can be able to abort the call and missions of God. It is a spirit that is from ancient days, from the time of Elijah. It's that same Jezebel that intervened when Ahab wanted his neighbor's land, and he asked to purchase it. When they refused, Jezebel intervened and caused the death of Nahab; his body was eaten by dogs. The land was then taken away under the power of the kingdom. The spirit uses this ability to destroy innocent lives. Sometimes innocent men like Ahab are married to Jezebel, and because of the influence of Jezebel, it caused Ahab to be weak-willed and to operate unethically.

Influence, manipulation, and control are the strongest traits of Jezebel's nature. These are spirits of witchcraft and are extremely dangerous. The spirit is a manipulator. It has a goal in mind. It is a good planner. It can plan for years to accomplish its mission. Jezebel must be in dominion. This spirit is extremely bossy. She is easily offended if her authority is questioned. It's an incorrigible spirit that cannot be corrected.

She operates like a mini goddess. Everybody must bow down to her when she enters a room. She likes the attention. She likes to be seen. You are in a no-win situation with Jezebel. Nothing pleases the spirit. She is a perfectionist and sets unrealistic expectations for others. The Jezebel spirit uses other people as objects to gain control, influence, and power. Once that control is gained, she kicks those people to the curb. If someone gains a favorable reputation with the person she's manipulating, she tries to sabotage that relationship with character assassination. Jezebel wants to be on top. She knows it all. She has that obsessive passion for power so that people have to bow down to her knowledge.

Jezebel can be a man or a woman. It's a spirit, so it doesn't even matter. It's neutral in this gender. It's a spirit that the enemy uses in society in today's world. She tries to destroy a person's reputation in order to gain control and undermine authority. She's very proud; she hides in false humility. But in the same breath, she is very proud, condescending, and lacks submission.

The Bible talks about submission as a characteristic of a wife that she must be submissive to her husband. It says in Ephesians 5:22-33, "[22]Wives, submit yourselves unto your own husbands, as unto the Lord. [23] For the husband is the head of the wife, even as Christ is the head of the church: and he is the savior of the body. [24] Therefore, as the church is subject unto Christ, so let the wives be to their own husbands in every thing. [25]Husbands love your wives, even as Christ also loved the church, and gave himself for it; [26]That he might sanctify and cleanse it with the washing of water by the word, [27]That he might present it to himself a glorious church, not having spot, or wrinkle, or any such thing; but that it should be holy and without blemish. [28] So ought men to love their wives as their own bodies. He that loveth his wife loveth himself. [29] For no man ever yet hated his own flesh; but nourisheth and cherisheth it, even as the Lord the church: [30] For we are members of his body, of his flesh, and of his bones. [31] For this cause shall a man leave his father and mother and shall be joined unto his wife, and they two shall be one flesh. [32] This is a great mystery: but I speak concerning Christ and the church. [33] Nevertheless let every one of you in particular so love his wife even as himself, and the wife see that she reverence her husband."

Jezebel's spirit is also a lustful spirit. It lusts for power, and it tries to manifest itself in marriage. It manifests in various things like withholding sexual union from your husband for manipulative purposes and utilizing sexual temptation to draw one more powerful into a compromising position that will cause his destruction or downfall. You're not supposed to withhold sex from your partner, and whenever you do that, you are operating under the spirit of Jezebel.

Jezebel causes people to use defense mechanisms to get what they want, is very vicious, and sometimes displays violent behavior when opposed; she will turn and refuses to submit, especially if she has been successful at manipulating others in the past. You may say one thing to Jezebel, and she twists the very conversation in a manipulative way and makes you look like you are a wicked or cruel person. Jezebel tries to deceive to showcase themself by making untruths true in order to paint a good image of herself.

Jezebel likes to picture herself as better than other people. The spirit is a conniving spirit. She likes to swear. She likes to curse. She likes to use a superiority complex over folks in order to gain control. She likes to complain and murmur and criticize other people. She displays vicious manipulation and uses anger to gain control of a situation. People loosely talk about energy. They like to say that you have bad energy because they want to deplete the very thought of yourself in order to gain control over you.

Jezebel's spirits are very bitter and resentful. They try to victimize you. She has a lot of bitterness inside of her spirit that grows like cancer. It causes her to become even worse. She'll cry; she'll foam and fuss. She only can be around people who have bad morals and people whose lifestyle is not up to par. Jezebel is a dangerous spirit to be around. Many times she uses self-pity, her own weakness, to manipulate others. She tries to emotionally damage you. Jezebel loves to curse and to bring damnation on herself. The spirit of Jezebel is the master of criticizing and complaining. Jezebel has a superiority complex. She feels that she's intellectually and spiritually superior to others and loves to despise others.

Jezebel is very power-hungry. Jezebel feels like she's superior to anyone. She tries to attain power, but there's no power like the Holy Spirit. The Bible says in Acts Chapter 1, "But ye shall receive power, after that the Holy Ghost has come upon you: and ye shall be witnesses unto me both in Jerusalem, and in all Judaea, and in

Samaria, and unto the uttermost part of the earth." I want to say that this power, the greatest power somebody can attain, is from the Holy Spirit.

Jezebel roams around, looking for disciples for herself. She looks for people with the same spirit. She finds those who are weak, wounded, and in rebellion to work with them. Jezebel is a wind of confusion. She has a "give me" mentality. She draws her strength from controlling others. She spiritually drains her victims. She uses flaws and weaknesses. She uses fear, trepidation, and intimidation to control others. She sometimes uses prayer and God's name to create the illusion that she fears God. You have to be wary of people who are trying to gain a reputation by associating with people of power and prominence. Jezebel likes to get up to the top, but she cannot stay up there because she has no morals, no integrity; her spirit is wrong.

You have to know that you are warned against Jezebel's principles, against powers, against the rulers of the darkness of this world, against spiritual wickedness in high places. Ephesians 6:14 says you must take on the whole armor of God, that he may be able to stand in the evil days wearing the loins girt of truth, having on the breastplate of righteousness and the feet shot with the preparation of the gospel of peace. You have to know that we are fighting against Jezebel, we're fighting against principalities, we're fighting against powers. We're fighting against rulers of the darkness of this world.

Jezebel allowed Nabal to be eaten by dogs or his blood to be licked by dogs. But the prophet Elijah prophesied her end. She was eaten by dogs when thrown down by Jehu. She was subdued by the enemy; the dogs ate her flesh. Only her skull, hands, and feet were left. It's the same Jezebel, the wife of Ahab, who God allowed her to receive what she sowed. You can never sow peas and reap corn; whatsoever seed a man sows that shall he also reap. It is good to sow into humility; it is good to sow into the things of God because if you sow to the flesh, you shall reap corruption. But if you sow of the spirit, then of the spirit, you shall reap life and life forevermore.

Those are the traits of a Jezebel spirit, and we must identify her and erase her from our territory.

## Characteristics of a Believer

Submission is one of the traits of the believer. It causes you to be submissive. In other words, it means to be humble, to allow your husband to rule, or allow your husband not to be a manipulator, but to be in charge. Allow your husband to lead even if you know more than him, you work with your husband, but he is the leader; he's the captain. You're the first officer, the co-pilot, but you have to learn how to work with your husband.

You can't allow the Jezebel spirit to take full control of your life so that you manipulate your husband and take control of him. And when he's not in that capacity, you try to use his reputation to try to subjugate him, trying to allow him to be put in a place of defeat.

You are there to help your husband. You can't allow the Jezebel spirit to take control of you and to allow you to cause your husband to look like he's a nobody. That is a controlling spirit. That is a spirit of deceit, the spirit of manipulation, the spirit of pride that causes a woman or man to operate in a condescending Jezebel-controlling spirit.

We don't want that spirit in our marriages. We can't allow these Jezebel spirits to be in control when God has not put it that way. The man is the head of the woman.

## Repent and Be Watchful

Jezebel is a very unrepentant person, and anytime somebody comes to the place of being unrepentant, it is dangerous ground. It's not a good place to be. Whenever you have a repentant heart, that is a safe ground with God. Romans 1 talks about folks who are unrepentant; the Jezebel spirit can lead you into a certain lifestyle and marriage.

It says in Romans 1:18-32, *"18For the wrath of God is revealed from heaven against all ungodliness and unrighteousness of men, who hold the truth in unrighteousness; 19Because that which may be known of God is manifest in them; for God hath showed it unto* them. [20]For the invisible things of him from the creation of the world are clearly seen, being understood by the things that are made, even his eternal power and Godhead; so that they are without excuse: [21]Because that, when they knew God, they glorified him not as God, neither were thankful; but became vain in their imaginations, and their foolish heart was darkened. [22]Professing themselves to be wise, they became fools, [23]And changed the glory of the incorruptible God into an image made like to corruptible man, and to birds, and four-footed beasts, and creeping things. [24]Wherefore God also gave them up to uncleanness through the lusts of their own hearts, to dishonor their own bodies between themselves: [25]Who changed the truth of God into a lie, and worshipped and served the creature more than the Creator, who is blessed forever. Amen. [26]For this cause God gave them up unto vile affections: for even their women did change the natural use into that which is against nature: [27]And likewise also the men, leaving the natural use of the woman, burned in their lust one toward another; men with men working that which is unseemly, and receiving in themselves that recompense of their error which was meet. [28]And even as they did not like to retain God in their knowledge, God gave them over to a reprobate mind, to do those things which are not convenient; [29]Being filled with all unrighteousness, fornication, wickedness, covetousness, maliciousness; full of envy, murder, debate, deceit, malignity; whisperers, [30]Backbiters, haters of God, despiteful, proud, boasters, inventors of evil things, disobedient to parents, [31]Without understanding, **covenant breakers**, without natural affection, implacable, unmerciful: [32]Who knowing the judgment of God, that they which commit such things are worthy of death, not only do the same, but have pleasure in them that do them."

Romans 2:1-2 continues, "[1]Therefore thou art inexcusable, O man, whosoever thou art that judgest: for wherein thou judgest another, thou condemnest thyself; for thou that judgest doest the same things. [2] But we are sure that the judgment of God is according to truth against them which commit such things."

I want to emphasize that there are certain lifestyles that God may allow to lead you into a reprobate mind, similar to what happened to Jezebel, and being in that state is a perilous place to be, particularly without repentance.

It's a dangerous place to stand being unrepentant in the body of Christ. Don't allow the Jezebel spirit to control your marriage, your mind, or your surrounding. Don't allow it to make you a deceiver, a man-hater, power-hungry, self-worshiping, jealous, and manipulative. Don't allow Jezebel spirits to come upon you and to possess your life and allow you to do things outside of God's will and God's nature. Don't allow Jezebel to conquer you and allow you to walk out of the will of God.

Jezebel is a wicked unrepentant spirit that hates marriage. It's a spirit that hates the kingdom of God. It does not like you when you are doing the things of God; it calls you all kinds of names. It will call you weird. It'll call you bad energy. It opposes that which concerns God. It caused the same prophet that called down fire from heaven. She sent over that threat, and Elijah was shaken up by this very prophetess named Jezebel. It has a spirit of intimidation. it'll intimidate you and cause you to become weary.

But my scripture says, be not weary in well-doing for in due season you shall reap if we faint not. You have to stand your ground as it relates to Jezebel. Don't allow Jezebel to be in control of you. Don't allow Jezebel to take manipulative powers over your life and try to minimize and mitigate you. Don't allow Jezebel to be in full reign and ruin your life or be destructive over you. Don't allow Jezebel to be a God over your life.

You have to know how to stand in the test of time and allow God to fight for you. Because if God is for you, if God is for your marriage, who can be against you? Folks will try to deceive and to belittle you and to hold you back. But when God is ready, God blesses you above the nature and thinking of man, and they won't be able to stop what God has promised and purposed for your life. **The purpose will stand the test of time.** You have to know that God is with you.

Jezebel cannot stop what God has purposed. Jezebel cannot stop what God has made. Jezebel cannot stop what God has called. Jezebel cannot stop what God has put into effect because there is the spirit of Elijah that's standing in the gap; irrespective of what Jezebel has done, God says, I'm coming through on your behalf. I'm stopping the mouth of the lion. I'm stopping every attack of the enemy. Anything that the enemy meant for bad God is turning it around and making it good. You have to stand amidst your circumstances. Amidst everything, the Bible said, out of your bellies shall flow rivers of living water. You have to allow that water and that river to flow through you so that it will not become stagnant and become a place where Jezebel can dwell.

Don't allow those spirits to dwell and to come and fester upon what God has promised in your life. The hand of God has called you in such a time as this, and if God calls you, nobody can stop him. Because the songwriter said, if I hold my peace and let the Lord fight my battles, victory shall be mine. Victory shall be yours today. If you learn how to hold your peace and let God fight and tear down the stronghold of Jezebel because the scripture says for you, wrestle not against flesh and blood. It says though we walk in the flesh, we do not war after the flesh, for the weapons of our warfare are mighty through God to the pulling down of any stronghold that Jezebel has set up.

We commend the strongholds of Jezebel to be torn down. We command every foothold of Jezebel to collapse. We command every foot of Jezebel, wherever it is, to come to naught because God must get the glory in your life. God must get the glory. **Your marriage is the most sacred and important part of your life.** You have to learn how to allow God to fight your battles. The enemy may be like a flood, but the spirit of God will lift up a standard against him.

## Trust God

There are many spirits out there in the world, and you have to realize that if you lean on the things of God, those spirits won't be able to stop you. Those spirits won't be able to hold you back and to tie you up and to hold back what God has purposed. Those spirits will not be able to alter the plan of God in your life. If you learn how to trust in the hand of God, it's just a matter of time; God is going to come through. You may not know how, you may not know when, but he's going to do it again because Jezebel has no power over God.

You have to know that if God is on your side, nothing can stop God. Nothing can thwart or destroy his very plan. God is in control of everything. Everything that God says will come to pass in their life. The voodoo people can't stop it; the sorcerers, the wizards can't stop it. Astro travel, yogis can't stop it; fortune tellers, witchcraft, or obeah men can't stop it. The juju man can't stop it; whatever it is, **they cannot stop what God has a purpose in your life.**

## Self-Examination

I want you to examine yourself. Is there a Jezebel spirit that has been bothering you, harassing you, tormenting you, and trying to belittle your power and authority in God?

I want you to understand that with the inspirational knowledge of God, I come to tell you to have power over every Jezebel spirit, over every discouraging demon, over every principality, over every prince demon. You have that power. So stand up over Jezebel.

God is the most important being known to man. If you draw nigh unto God, he will draw nigh onto you. I want to embrace you today that if you begin to draw nigh to God, every evil force of Jezebel has to back off everything that seems like it's trying to tie you up and to hold you back. Every spirit of unbelief, rejection, infirmity, lawlessness, deception, pride, heresy, domineering, fear; every schizophrenic spirit, every spirit of blockage, lust, every spirit of Jezebel has to back off when God is ready to bless you and to take the full authority and to take full preeminence.

But you have to know, as long as you know who you are dealing with, then you are a hundred percent ahead in the race. You know that the victories are already won, and the battles are already fought. You already know that you have the power to control and to abort and to break and to take and tear down the walls of Jezebel in and through the lives of the people. I promise you, Jezebel, cannot stop the promises of God in the believer's life or in their marriage.

## Traits of Jezebel

- Seeks to control, influence, and dominate men.

- Has an unnatural sense of self-importance.

- Requires excessive admiration and attention.

- Falsely accuses men of God and desires to destroy them.

- Lacks self-control and is unable to control emotional outbursts.

- She is really manipulative and takes advantage of others to achieve her goals.

- Jealous and envious of anyone who is a threat to her.

- Defensive when confronted.

- She lacks genuine empathy but will fake empathy to seduce and control her victims.

- Has a sense of entitlement and demands

Jezebel and her manipulation is being muzzled at this very moment. I saw a glimpse of the attack you have been under, the lies, accusations, and control that spirit has been deploying in your life - it ends today in Jesus' name!

# CHAPTER 7

## FATHERS IN MARRIAGE

*"¹Now the LORD had said unto Abram, Get thee out of thy country, and from thy kindred, and from thy father's house, unto a land that I will shew thee: ²And I will make of thee a great nation, and I will bless thee, and make thy name great; and thou shalt be a blessing: ³And I will bless them that bless thee, and curse him that curseth thee: and in thee shall all families of the earth be blessed."*

*Genesis 12:1-3*

*"¹Blessed is every one that feareth the LORD; that walketh in his ways. ²For thou shalt eat the labor of thine hands: happy shalt thou be, and it shall be well with thee. ³Thy wife shall be as a fruitful vine by the sides of thine house: thy children like olive plants round about thy table. ⁴Behold, that thus shall the man be blessed that feareth the LORD. ⁵The LORD shall bless thee out of Zion: and thou shalt see the good of Jerusalem all the days of thy life. 6Yea, thou shalt see thy children's children and peace upon Israel."*

*Psalms 128*

## Fathers

I t certainly takes a lot of work to be a father. It is a process of development to be a father. "Father" is a stronger word than even "daddy"; it is a word that fortifies the responsibility of a man who is married and has children. It also fortifies the responsibilities of a man who gets children apart from being a "sugar daddy." Having a child is an easy task for a man. But raising one is a harder task. You have to possess responsible traits. In order to be a true father, you have to have a lifetime commitment as a man to protect, cover, and provide for your family. To be a true father, you have to maintain the figure of a true father for life; that is, raising your child through school, church, college, and through all the vicissitudes of life. Every child is a potential seed of greatness. It will take a community to raise that child.

A father is like a farmer. A farmer is knowledgeable and proficient enough to know his environment and where he wants to plant his seed for his harvest. For the seed to be well, he has to know how to cultivate the plant in the nursery for it to grow and prosper. God has placed every person in every family strategically. He has set them to live a life of purpose to fulfill their destiny. No matter what it is in life, everything has a purpose. God himself knows the end from the beginning. There are rewards for your faithfulness. There are many benefits to what you are aspiring for in life.

The book of Psalms is filled with a lot of promises, a lot of prophecies, and a lot of proclamations. The book of Psalms is a complement of different authors. It has 150 books, mostly written by the Psalmist David. However, according to theologians, Psalm chapter 128, a song of decrees, the author of which is unknown, is very profound on families and speaks about the family structure. Everything shall be well concerning your family.

## Father Abraham

I want to look at one of the Patriots in the Bible; the first father, one of the greatest fathers around, Father Abraham. We spoke about him in Genesis chapter 12, which talks about the call of Abram. That was his first name until God changed it to Abraham, which means "the father of many." Abraham was married to Sarah, and they had no children together. Abraham was a great patriot when God called Abraham. God said to him, get thee out of thy land, out of thy father's house, into the land that I will show thee. Abraham was a man of great faith. He obeyed God and went in the direction that God had for him.

God promised him and said, "I will bless you." You see, when God says that he's going to do something for you, you can rely on it. God is not a man that he should lie to. When God promises you, he will bring it to pass. So God said unto Abraham, "I'll bless you, and I will make you a great nation, and I'll make thy name great." God promised them law, land, and posterity. God promised Abraham a people and that He will bless them.

Abraham was called by God to live in a new land. God said, get thee out of thy father's house. Many of us are in our comfort zones, and God wants to take us out of our comfort zone to bless us. We are too comfortable depending on others to provide for us. God wants to take us out of that comfort zone in order to provide and show us that he is God. Abraham became the Father of Israel. Abraham lived for about 175 years. His wife, Sarah, lived until about 127 years old and had their sons in their old age.

While God had promised Abraham something, God told him to go into the land, and He will show him. Abraham brought his nephew, named Lot. He never knew that Lot would have been a problem. They had a conflict, and Abraham sent Lot into the better place, and he took a smaller place for himself. Genesis 14:14 mentions that Abraham sent out 318 men to fight the four kings that went out against them. They won the battle, and the King of Sodom wanted to give Abraham gifts, but Abraham said to him, No, I don't need your blessing; keep it.

I will tell you this now, the blessing of man does not make you rich; it has many sorrows with it. But when God blesses you, you are blessed and prosperous. Some will be blessed to the point where they become the greatest in their family, inspiring jealousy. Therefore, the jealous will try to tear them down. But when God blesses you, your name will be great. All of us want greatness to our name, we want titles, and we want PhDs behind our name. But when your name is great, you don't need anything behind your name. All you need is God. People are fighting for titles, but a good name is better than money. When you have a good name that can defend you, that name goes before you.

Greater is he that's in Me than he that is in the world. We call him Jesus. We call everybody reverend, doctor, bishop, but we call Him Jesus. Why? Because that name is greater. The name above every name. That name shall confess that Jesus is Lord. God promised Abraham and said, I will make your name great, and I will bless you. He said I will multiply thy seeds as the stars in heaven. God is a God of multiplicity. When God promises to bless you, He will bless the socks off of your feet. You will be blessed like you've never been blessed without limits. A songwriter said, no limits, no boundaries. I see increasing all around me.

## God's Blessings

Only God can bless me, and God will use man to bless you. Sometimes people are being used by God to bless you. "I will bless them that bless you," He said. They, in turn, are getting their own blessing. It's not about them but about a God who's using them to bless you, and they will be blessed. That is the Abrahamic covenant. People need to be careful when they come against a child of God. There's a blessing of reciprocity that multiplies and the law of returns. Whatever it is, if it is good, it shall return; if it's bad, it shall return. You better be careful when touching God's child; touch not my anointed and do my prophets no harm.

Some people come and take the pastor for granted because the pastor is so humble. But, I tell you that he is God's man, and when you bless him, God will bless you. When you do the opposite, God will do the opposite. He said, "I'll bless them that will bless you." So it is not man who gets the glory, but God who gets the glory in everything. Paul the Apostle said God causes all things to grow. God gets the glory; the increase comes from God. Man cannot set up blessings. They can't hang it over your head. If your boss comes and calls you and says, "I'm going to give you a promotion," that did not come from him; it came from God.

When Pharaoh had the dream, that did not come from Him, it came from God. The heart of the king is in the hand of the Lord and turns it. When God blesses you, nobody can curse you. Do not care about what they do or what they say. They can't block your blessing. They can put a barrel in the way, put a block in the way, put a truck in the way; whatever it is, you will leap over it. You will rise above everything; the devil can't stop you because the devil is a liar. He has no validity.

If Satan promises you something, you will not get it. If he gives you something, he is going to take it back. But when God gives you something, He doesn't take it back. The callings of God are irrevocable without repentance, so even when you "backslide," God still will bless you. He's still looking for a way for you to come back to Him for the goodness of the Lord. So God, in Psalm 128, said that He's going to bless you. He said, "Blessed is every one that feareth the Lord, that walketh in his ways."

In Psalm 1:1-3, he said,

*"¹Blessed is the man that walketh not in the counsel of the ungodly, nor standeth in the way of sinners, nor sitteth in the seat of the scornful. ²But his delight is in the law of the LORD; and in his law doth he meditate day and night. ³And he shall be like a tree planted by the rivers of water, that bringeth forth his fruit in his season; his leaf also shall not wither; and whatsoever he doeth shall prosper..."*
*Psalm 1:1-3*

You can't go before your season. You can't go before your time. Weeping may endure for a night, but joy comes in the morning. Everything is a time and season. The season of sorrow is about to be over. The season of waiting is about to be over.

## Fear

There are two kinds of fear. One is reverence, and the other is respect. When it comes to God, there must be some kind of reverence. When you go to the courtroom, you have to stand when the judge enters. You can't be talking; you can't be chewing guns. You can't be doing certain things out of order. The judge will reprimand you or even put you in jail. We have so much order in the courtroom, but when it comes to God's court, the church, we do anything that we want to do, we talk, we criticize the pastor, we do all sorts of things. We need some fear in the house of God.

Peter said, "Your life, not onto men, but your life to the Holy Ghost." That is the kind of fear we need in the house of God; we need to fear God. As a person, you should fear God than fear man. The fear of man brings a snare, but when you fear God, you will be blessed. You operate according to his precepts. God is a God of order and principle. God wants to bless you. Your life has to be in order first. You must set your house in order for God to bless you.

You have to fear and be reverent in the house of God. Put God's things first. Respect God's people. Respect the ushers. Respect the pastor. Respect everything. Everything has to be in order, decently and in order. He said, "For thou shall eat the labor of thine hands, happy thou shalt be, and it will be well with thee." Many people are eating from other people's hands; we borrow, we beg, we steal, but God is saying, I want to bless you with your own hands. I want to bless you; you shall eat from the labor of your own hands, your own work. From your own hands shall you eat, not from another man's hands; you shall be the head and not the tail.

## Happy and Blessed

The word "happy" means "blessed." Blessing is not what you have; it's not connected to your possessions. Blessing is the contentment of your heart. It's not the amount of money that you have; it's the contentment of your heart, and how happy your heart is that is what makes you blessed. Many people walk around with "bling bling," but they're not happy; they're not blessed. But when happiness hits you, you're satisfied with anything, especially when God is in it.

So many times, we judge being blessed by looking at what other people have. But that is covetousness, that is envy, that is jealousy, that is greed, that is pride. Don't look at what other people have to determine your blessing. Your life is set for you. Stay on your track and run in your lane, don't deviate, and watch God bless you. If you're distracted, you'll lose a blessing. Look for the prize. Look ahead of you. Don't turn around. Look for what God has in store for you. Stay focused, and stay blessed. Stop watching your friends. Your friends will stop you from being blessed. Look ahead of you and see your blessing.

You see, you cannot "chase two rabbits" at the same time. You're going to rip yourself apart. You cannot serve God and man at the same time. You can't serve God and the devil at the same time. You got to focus on one person, one thing, one Him. Many people come, and they try to do everything in the church. We try to do everything at the same time. We're not focused. So what happened? There's no target. But if we take one success at a time, one goal at a time, one mission at a time, we will accomplish something. Count your blessings one by one, and it will surprise you what the Lord has done.

When God promised Abraham, Abraham was about 75 years old, and he waited until he was a hundred years old to get Isaac. Now within that transition, that period of waiting, there was a lot of pain, and his wife suggested he use the maid Hagar to produce a son, and that son became Ishmael. When God promises you, don't look left nor right; stay with the promise of God. Don't try to make this thing up. Don't try to put things together. Stay with what God has for you.

## The Devil's Mirage

There was a story about a greedy dog that lost his bone. He had a beautiful big bone in his mouth. He looked into a pool of water, and he saw a shinier bone. The bone looked bigger, and what did this dog do? He let go of his bone to get the bone, and it fell into the water. In doing so, he lost his big bone and got nothing.

The devil always has a mirage. He always has something there to distract you from what God has for you. When God tells you something, stay focused. Your blessing is right here. It's right before you, but you have to stay focused. Remember what God has promised you, and remember His promise to Abraham. God came down and promised Abraham, by this time next year, you shall produce a son and a son of promise, which is Isaac. God gave him Isaac. When God promises, no matter what comes, no matter the mistakes you make, he will bring forth His promise.

## He That Finds a Wife

He goes on to say, "Thy wife shall be as a fruitful vine by the sides of thine house." How powerful! Solomon said he who finds a wife finds a good thing and obtains favor of the Lord. Now, in order to get that wife, you have to have favor from God. Many women are out there, but not every woman is a wife. There are beautiful women, Attractive women, educated women, women who are up there in class, but none of them is a wife. Consider the source, Solomon; Solomon had many wives and concubines, but he said he that findeth a wife findeth a good thing and obtains favor from the Lord. Favor is something that is unmerited, it's a special blessing that comes from God, and you have to set yourself in a position for this to happen.

Some men want to get married, and they have nothing in place. You have to set things in place first. You want a wife to take care of you, but no, you must take care of her. God made Eve for Adam; Adam was in charge. And he was there to take care of the woman. She can work, but for him to take care of her. A lot of people want to get married, but nothing is in place.

Someone said all I have to give is love, but do you think love is enough? When hard times come, when the tribulations come, when the tough times come, will "love" keep you? Sometimes you're overshadowed by emotions, and there's no more love. So ladies, don't be fooled if he says, "All I have to give you is love," something is wrong with that. Watch the men who talk a lot. Some women are attracted to words. Perhaps also tall, dark, and handsome, yes, but sometimes I look at some wives and some husbands and think, "Oh my God, how he managed to get her." I would love to find his resources. I'd love to find what he has because it works. We should have a class that teaches men how to talk to women, charm classes.

## A Foundation For Marriage

Wisdom makes a man's face shine. Solomon, he had a lot of wisdom, a lot of words. Every girl he saw, he had the wisdom to speak and made them his wife. How you speak, your mannerisms, and so on, is not enough. You have to have structure. You have to have things in place so it doesn't backfire down the road. You're looking for a long-term investment. You're looking for something ahead of you, and in order to make this thing work, you have to have the foundation set properly. If the foundation is not set, the building is going to crack. When the foundation is not good, the house is not good. Knock it down and reset the foundation. You must have that foundation in place.

Children are like olive plants around their tables. Put your wife first, then the children, not the other way around. You don't go make kids out there, and then you get married. No, you get married first, and then you produce children. Your children shall be blessed. Your children shall be like olive plants. Olive is a blessed plant that produces olive oil, and you shall be blessed around that table.

Behold that thus shall the man be blessed that fears the Lord. The Lord shall bless thee out of Zion, and thou shall see the good of Jerusalem all the days of thy life. You shall see good in your house, in your church all the days of your life. Not for one day. Not for one week. Not for one year, but all the days of your life.

When God builds your foundation, and it sets, you shall see goodness all the days of your life. Yea, thou shall see thy children's children and peace upon Israel. God is promising somebody long life, so you shall see your children's children, your grandchildren. The blessing shall go on to the third and then to the fourth generation of them that fear Him. God's about to put some generational blessings down the line. God's about to give you a blessing like you've never seen blessings before.

# CHAPTER 8

## MARRIAGE AND THE FAVOR OF GOD

*"Whoso findeth a wife findeth a good thing, and obtaineth favor of
the Lord."*
*Proverbs 18:22*

The word favor comes from the word "grace," which means
"unmerited favor." Acceptance and love received from another, favor is God and of God, providing salvation for sinners.
For Christians, the word "grace" is virtually synonymous with the
gospel of God's gift of salvation in Jesus Christ. To express this,
New Testament writers use the Greek word "Charis," which has a
long history in secular Greek. Charis refers to something delightful
and attractive in a person, which brings pleasure to others. From
this, it came to have an idea of kindness done to another or a gift
that brought pleasure to another.

Favor is God's gift of grace toward humans in undeserving circumstances. Favor is that special act of kindness towards us when
things have surpassed or reached their limit.

In this world, which is so unstable and volatile, there is a profound need for God's special favor. Favor is God's ability to override the hopeless judgment towards us. We were a people lost and heading toward God's judgment, but because of God's favor were able to have salvation and the promise of eternal life. This is the same favor that is present with the grace of God that brings salvation.

## Favor "Ain't" Fair

I want to say today, favor "ain't" fair. The Bible says God commendeth his love towards us in that while we were yet sinners, Christ died for us. That's unfair because some people have done the same wrong, yet they have received the opposite punishment.

Favor "ain't" fair because you are at the back of the embassy line, and all of a sudden, someone took you to the front while others were waiting five hours in line. That's not fair. Favor "ain't" fair because God healed you from your disease, and someone else had to pay one hundred thousand dollars in medical bills, and still, they are not healed. That's not fair.

Favor "ain't" fair because you paid coach price and sat in first class on the 747 Boeing to Hawaii while others paid full price. That's not fair. Favor ain't fair because God called you gifted; you skipped the rules while others waited 13 years for that position. That's not fair. Favor "ain't" fair because God got you a promotion in two years while others have been there for 30 years on the same job, and that's not fair.

Favor "ain't" fair because some people went to the seminary to learn how to preach and teach while God graced you, gifted you supernaturally to teach and preach His word. That's still not fair. Favor "ain't" fear because you went into that dealership, no money, no credit, and came back out with that Mercedes-Benz, with that Honda, Accord, whatever it may be. That's still not fair.

Favor "ain't" fear because you are living in that one-room shack with no kitchen, no dining room, and all of a sudden, God blesses you with your big mansion. That's still not fair. Favor "ain't" fair because you couldn't read and write, but you now can interpret scriptures. That's still not fair. Favor "ain't" fair because you were never married, never had kids, never met anybody, but all of a sudden, you meet an attorney and get married. Now you have twins and triplets. That's still not fair.

Favor "ain't" fair because you sinned against God and brought the punishment of death, but Jesus canceled it and brought forth life saying, I am the resurrection, and I'm the life. Oh, that's still not fair. Favor "ain't" fair because Abraham lied to the King about Sarah, yet God made him Father of many nations. Favor "ain't" fair because Joseph was an ex-convict out of prison. Yet God made him prime minister over Egypt. Still not fair.

Favor "ain't" fair because Noah was a drunkard, yet God made a covenant with him, and blessed him greatly. Still not fair. Favor "ain't" fair because Moses was a murderer, yet God made him leader over Egypt, over Israel. Still not fair. Favor "ain't" fair because David was the biggest adulterer, biggest sham, and biggest murderer, yet God loved him and blessed him and made him a mighty king. Favor "ain't" fair because Solomon had more wives than I have suits. Yet God counted him blessed, counted him wise, and gave him the book of Proverbs. Still not fair.

## Favor Comes at Any Time

God doesn't look at your present circumstance to determine what He's about to do because he's an omniscient God; He's an all-knowing God. You may be at the bottom now, but God's about to flip the script. Turn it around and bless you because it's still not fair. When Satan judges you, and say you won't make it, and all hope is lost. But all of a sudden, God comes in, turns it around, and puts light before you because he's an all-powerful God. He's omnipotent; He's powerful, and He is mighty.

The devil said you're lost; you're bound. It seemed like you were leaning on your own understanding. It seems like you were never going to push forward, but all of a sudden, God gave you wisdom, insight, and vision. He made something turn in your life, and as a God that we serve, God can raise a nobody and make him "a somebody" because he's God and God all by himself.

Think about David. He was there in the depths of the wilderness, serving God all these years in faithfulness with a true heart. The Bible says God loved him. He was a man after God's own heart. I looked at David, Solomon's father, who served God in the wilderness by serving the animals, being a sheep keeper. He kept all those sheep, but all of a sudden, God sought him out in the remote wilderness.

Sometimes you feel you have reached nowhere, it seems like you are nobody, but all of a sudden, God looks for you. God knows where to find you. It doesn't matter where you are. God knows your circumstances. He knows your faithfulness. He knows what you're going through, and he knows just when to find you.

All of us came up before the prophet Samuel, but none of them could match the description that God had. I tell you this now; God has your description. God has your name written down. For all your faithfulness over the years, God has it written down in a book, and someday God's going to show up. He's going to look for you. You don't have to move from where you are. Stay in your position because God knows where to find you.

You may be deep in a dark wilderness, but God knows where and how to find you. Just remain humble, stay steadfast, unmovable, always abounding in the work of the Lord; you know that your labor is not in vain in the Lord. God knew where to find David. Sometimes you're tied up with some animals. Sometimes you're deep in the wilderness.

David had to encounter many things in the depths of the wilderness. He was not in a king's palace. He wasn't trained in a king's court, but he was down in the wilderness, and here came the lion. He was able to defeat the lion. Sometimes your circumstance is preparing you for what's ahead, so remain with God because all of a sudden, favor is going to show up at your door. It may be mail that you're about to get; maybe a phone call, favor is about to show up. Your blessing is about to arrive. Don't move, don't shift.

Favor is about to show somebody who said you wouldn't get it, somebody who said you wouldn't make it. All of a sudden, favor will show up. That's the God I serve because favor is not fair. The Bible says man looks on outward appearances, but God looks at the heart. Man looks at his height or his stature, but God looks from the heart. God watches your faithfulness, so remain faithful. God is about to bless you. He's about to bless the socks off your feet when you remain faithful.

## The Parable of the Talents

I looked at Matthew chapter 25, Jesus spoke a parable about a man who had servants. He gave them talents, left, and went into a far country. The Bible says he gave one five talents. He gave the other two talents, and he gave one a talent. The Bible said he took a long time to come back. Now talent in this context represents money. When he came back, one that he gave five, he doubled it a hundred percent. The one he gave two talents got two more, which made it four. But the one he gave one talent, he did nothing with that talent. He hid it and gave it back to the master, and yet he complained. Now, the master was upset, but he took away that one talent, and he gave it to the one who had ten talents, and he said to one who had one talent who did nothing with it, "You wicked and slothful servant."

My point is this; God is watching your faithfulness. Sometimes when God blesses somebody, we, with our finite minds, try to interpret the movements of God. However, God will often use a situation over many years to test your heart, and if you have been faithful over those few things, God will make you a master over many things. If you continue to remain steadfast and diligent over what God has placed in you, you will step into your promotion.

Sometimes in our finite mind, we may interpret it in our own way, but God is infinite and omniscient. He knows the end from the beginning; He has a book in which He writes everything down. And when God is ready to bless you and put you in your position, no man can stop it.

I look at the scripture in Psalm that says, "For promotion does not come from the east nor the west nor the south, but it comes from up north, from God." It comes from the Lord. So don't look for promotion among you, but look to Him, who is the author and the finisher of your faith. My scripture tells me that He, who has begun a good work in you, will perform it until the day of Jesus Christ.

God will open a door that no man can close. When God does it, it's done. When we do it, it's half done; but when God does it, it is complete. It's blessed. There's no failure with God. All you have is success. All you have is a blessing. All you have is goodness and mercies. My Bible says, surely goodness and mercies shall follow you all the days of your life when you have favor with God. You don't have to run after a blessing. It'll follow you.

God knows just where to find you. Favor is about locating somebody. Favor is about to locate you at your address. Favor is about doing something that you couldn't do for yourself. That's the God that we serve. Sometimes, you know, I question how God moves. Some people tend to be overly qualified for a job, but when somebody whom God has blessed with favor, somebody who has been praying to God, who God has been watching, their faithfulness steps in, gets that interview.

Your friend has been qualified for many years, and you don't even have a one-year's experience, but you sit down, and that person, the interviewer, sees that honesty inside you. They see something, they see potential, and God is speaking into their mind, and they have no other choice than to give you that position. They have no choice but to give you that job because it's God.

Scripture says, God turns the heart of the king; in the hand of the Lord, He turns it. God will speak to that manager. He's eternal, he's immortal, he's invisible, and he is the only wise God.

## Favor In Your Marriage

The favor of God is priceless. When you get or obtain favor from God, you have preferential "VIP treatment." It is Loyalty from the imperial majesty. Proverbs 18:22 declares; he who finds a wife finds a good thing and obtains favor from God. This favor is a special grace that comes with marriage.

When you are married, a greater favor comes with the territory. There is a greater sense of respect from man and with God. God honors marriage. The word of God says marriage is honorable, and the bed is undefiled. Marriage, indeed, is an honorable thing, and favor with privilege come with honor.

One of the privileges is to have clean sex. The next privilege is keeping your body pure with one person not being susceptible to STDs etc. Another privilege is having children born in wedlock. This wedlock birth is a special blessing that comes with a sanctified marriage.

One of the things God told Adam is that he should be fruitful & multiply and replenish the Earth and subdue it because children are a heritage of the Lord. The fruit of the womb is his reward. God wants to bless and favor the next generation through the lineage of marriage.

So favor is that special aura that comes with marriage. I found many more blessings in my life by being married.

I pray you will honor marriage so favor and understanding will emanate in and through you.

# CONCLUSION

The Grace and Love of God will grant you the strength to fulfill your purpose on Earth in marriage. The word of the Lord says; be fruitful and multiply and replenish the Earth. We are only to multiply in the context of marriage.

It takes the oil of God's grace to complete the painstaking journey and task set before us. Only God's grace in marriage can assist us in overcoming challenges and hurdles before us. Many times it may seem difficult and insurmountable. I hope that the word of God and these additional tools in "The Marriage Mechanic" can help give you the zest to push and leap over all obstacles and win your marriage through with Love, which passes all knowledge.

Often, we come to Christ with things we cannot undo. You often can't unscramble what is already done. However, God's grace will take you through, no matter the circumstances or situations. The Favor of God will help you make that turn and alignment with God's word.

I hope with "The Marriage Mechanic," you were able to make introspective and the necessary adjustments in your marriage and family relationships. I hope these precious tips were jewels to your eyes. I hope you are able to apply them and shine in your marital glory.

God Bless you.

# Appendix A: Marriage Vows

## Preface of the Marriage vow

This is what we consider a prelude to the marriage vow it starts:

"Dearly beloved, we are gathered here in the sight of God, and in the presence of these witnesses, to join together this man and this woman in holy matrimony; which is an honorable estate, instituted of God. It is therefore, not to be entered into unadvisedly, but reverently, discreetly, and in the fear of God."

# Appendix B: Marriage Poems & A Role Model Marriage

## A Poem To Remember by Wilferd A. Peterson.

This poem will ring in your ears very often.

### The Art of Marriage ~ Wilferd A. Peterson

The little things are the big things.
It is never being too old to hold hands.
It is remembering to say "|love you" at least once a day.
It's never going to sleep angry,
it is at no time taking the other for granted,
the courtship should not end with the honeymoon,
it should continue through all the years.
It is having a mutual sense of values and common objectives.
It is standing together facing the world.
It is forming a circle of love that gathers in the whole family.
It is doing things for each other.
Not in the attitude of duty or sacrifice, but in the spirit of joy.

It is speaking words of appreciation
and demonstrating gratitude in thoughtful ways.
It is not expecting the husband to wear a halo
or the wife to have wings of an angel.
It is not looking for perfection in each other.
It is cultivating flexibility, patience, understanding
and a sense of humor.
It is having the capacity to forgive and forget.
It is giving each other an atmosphere in which each can grow.
It is finding room for the things of the spirit.
It is a common search for the good and the beautiful.
It is establishing a relationship in which
the independence is equal, dependence is mutual
and the obligation is reciprocal.
It is not only marrying the right partner,
it is being the right partner.

## Blessed Hands

This poem shows the deep intimacy with the hands of your
partner.

### Blessed Hands ~ Unknown

These are the hand of your best friend,
Young and strong and full of love for you,
That are holding yours on your wedding day,

As you promise to love each other today, tomorrow, and forever.
These are the hands that will work alongside yours,
As you build your future.
These are the hands that will passionately love you
and cherish you through the years,
And with the slightest touch, will comfort you like no other.
These are the hands that will hold you when fear or
grief fills your mind.
These are the hands that will countless times wipes the
tears from your eyes, Tears of sorrow, and as today, tears of joy.
These are the hands that will tenderly hold your children,
The hands that will help you hold your family as one.
These are the hands that will give you strength
when you need it.
And lastly, these are the hands that even when wrinkled
and aged, will still be reaching for yours,
still giving you the same unspoken tenderness with just a touch.

Author Unknown

# A Role Model Marriage

-Carlington Wilmot

■ The Douglases go few places without each other.

## An old-fashioned love

D RS. JAMES and Roslyn Douglas, pastors of Christian Fellowship World Outreach, provide awe-inspiring use of religious community-based ministries in Kingston and St. Andrew. Those who are close to them also know that the couple are an inspiration to themselves.

Pastors and marriage counsellors, both, they espouse old-fashioned values, and a credit-size of life, without apologising for it. They state that these values have worked for them for forty-five years.

James, hailing from Kellits in Clarendon, and Roslyn from Aboukir in St. Ann, met by chance at a crusade near Race Course in Kingston. The year was 1956.

James was then a young evangelist. "I got saved under his ministry," Roslyn fondly recalls. It was love and a spiritual revival combined. The courtship lasted a short year. They got married in 1957. According to James, "As a young Christian, I desperately looked to the Lord. I wanted the person that He would want me to have." She (Roslyn) was pretty, she was neat. She was soft spoken. She was steadfast in her belief in the Lord." He laughs as he recalls this and adds, "She could not resist me. She could just not resist me."

Soon after getting married, the young couple received scholarships to attend the Zion Bible College in Barrington, Rhode Island, USA. Following graduation, they were ordained in the Pentecostal church, and together they launched their ministry.

The duo have has pastored several congregations, and have established the Christian Fellowship World Outreach at Dumfries Avenue in St. Andrew. They have been granted honorary doctorates in recognition of their work, their commitment

-Contributed

■ As young graduates of Zion Bible College, Barrington, Rhode Island, USA.

# An old-fashioned love

and accomplishments.

Their son, James, was born after 13 years of marriage. He was received with great gladness as a gift from the God they served.

The couple was awarded National Model Family in 1986/7.

Roslyn and James are qualified both by experience and training to dispense the marriage advice they give. Roslyn is in fact a marriage counsellor and has much to say on the reasons why newer marriages are weaker in Jamaica.

"Couples do not want to commit themselves to each other. The wife does not want to be obedient according to the word of God. Wives are supposed to be in subjection."

## Sharing and caring

Her husband, Rev Douglas, qualifies this. "They [couple] have not learnt the art of sharing and caring. The man is not over the woman like a boss, but there is a sharing of mutual love and respect. The key to a wife and husband living together successfully is forgiveness. Teeth and tongue will meet, but when it's dinner time, they must come together.

"There is an old-fashioned notion to have the wife as a helper. She is a help meet and this meeting is on mutual grounds. There are some men who believe that all the woman needs is money. There is no fellowship."

"Your husband is supposed to be your best friend," his wife advises, observing that a major stumbling block to successful relationships is communication, or the lack of it. Dr. Douglas adds, "The scripture says a man should leave father and mother and they together shall be one flesh. Both parties are often guilty of breaking this. The wife goes off to her parents and complains and the men do the same. It does not help the union. The parents will naturally treat the accused according to what they are told."

They, as a family, have tried to live by this. Cleaving is easier because Roslyn "has not gone out to work a day", her husband says. "We are always together whatever we do. We travel together abroad and here in Jamaica. We went to college together. I do not go out on nights [home visits]. We are [...]

together in the office and if functions I have never gone out with my friends and left out alone.

Finances also call for unity. Our problem, Rinh, a reverend, is that where the wife is working and earning a greater income than her husband, they [the couple] will not put resources together. In their family everything is shared. "Both our names are in one [bank] account. We do not hide anything from each other. Once you get married, you should begin to pool."

The husband and pastor adds, "That is why the marriage vow says that you should not enter marriage indiscreetly." His wife adds, "You cannot say this is mine". They get married but they have not come together."

"It is not that we have never had problems," she insists, "but the important thing is to think it over and learn to say 'I am sorry, please forgive me. I will try to see it never happens again'. Then, take it to the Lord and pray together. These are some of the things that will let marriage stick. Say, I love you. I appreciate you. I thank you. Your caring must be expressed."

The marriage counsellor notes that secrets also cause marriages to fall apart. The disclosure clause in the marriage vows should be taken more seriously, she states.

Dr. Douglas, as a community leader, is forced to make one admission.

## Challenge

"We cannot deny there is a different challenge today [compared to when they started].

"It is challenging to live up to, the Joneses. Try to be moderate. Live by principles. If not you will drift."

His wife gets the last word in. She concludes, "staying together has been a work of love. I love him for who he is and he loves me for who I am. The love of God is shed abroad, but, in the natural, if you do not love each other, you will not stay together."

Her husband agrees. "There is a love which is beyond the ordinary. I have never doubted my wife. I have never thought that she would have another man with me. I would never betray her. She would never betray me."

The feeling is mutual.

## "An old-fashioned love

Dr. James and Rev. Roslyn Douglas, pastors of Christian Fellowship World Outreach, presided over one of the strongest community-based institutions in Kingston and St. Andrew. Those who are close to them also know; that the couple is an institution in themselves.

Pastors and marriage counselors, both, they espouse old-fashioned values, and a Godly way of life, without apologizing for it. They state that these values have worked for them for forty-four years.

James, hailing from Kellits in Clarendon, and Roslyn from Aboukir in St. Ann, met by chance at a crusade near Race Course in Kingston. The year was 1956.

James was then a young evangelist. "I got saved under his ministry," Roslyn fondly recalls. It was love and a spiritual revival combined. The courtship lasted a short year. They got married in 1956.

According to James, "As a young Christian, I desperately looked to the Lord. I wanted the person that He would want me to have. She (Roslyn) was pretty; she was neat. She was soft-spoken. She was steadfast in her belief in the Lord." He laughs as he recalls this and adds, "She could not resist me. She could not say 'no'" Soon after getting married, the young couple received scholarships to attend the Zion Bible College in Barrington, Rhode Island,

USA. Following graduation, they were ordained in the Pentecostal church, and together they launched their ministry.

The two have pastored several congregations and have established the Christian Fellowship World Outreach at Dunrobin Avenue in St. Andrew. They have been granted honorary doctorates in recognition of their work, their commitment...

They Attended College in Barrington, Rhode Island, USA. Following graduation, they were ordained in the Pentecostal church, and together they launched their ministry and accomplishments.

Their son, James, was born after 13 years of marriage. He was received with great gladness as a gift from the God they served. The couple was awarded National Model Family in 1986/7.

Roslyn and James are qualified both by experience and training to dispense the marriage advice they give. Roslyn is, in fact, a marriage counselor and has much to say on the reasons why newer marriages are weaker in Jamaica. "Couples do not want to commit themselves to each other. The wife does not want to be obedient according to the word of God. Wives are supposed to be in subjection."

**Sharing and Caring**

Her husband, Rev Douglas, qualifies this. "They (couples) have not learnt the art of sharing and caring. The man is not over the woman like a boss, but there is a sharing of mutual love and respect. The key to a wife and husband living together successfully is forgiveness. Teeth and tongue will meet, but when it's dinner time, they must come together.

"There is an old-fashioned notion to have the wife as a helper. She is a help meet and this meeting is on mutual grounds. There are some men who believe that all the woman needs is money. There is no fellowship."

"Your husband is supposed to be your best friend," his wife advises, observing that a major stumbling block to successful relationships is communication or the lack of it. Dr. Douglas adds, 'The scripture says a man should leave father and mother and they together shall be one flesh. Both parties are often guilty of breaking this. The wife goes off to her parents and complains and the men do the same. It does not help the union. The parents will naturally treat the accused according to what they are told."

They, as a family, have tried to live by this. Cleaving is easier because Roslyn "has not gone out to work a day', her husband says. "We are always together whatever we do. We travel together abroad and here in Jamaica. We went to college together. I do not go out on night (home visits). We are together in the office and at functions. I have never gone out with my friends and left her alone."

Finances also call for unity.

One problem, Roslyn observes, is that where the wife is working and earning a greater income than her husband, they (the couple) will not put resources together. In their family, everything is shared. Both our names are in one (bank) account. We do not hide anything from each other. Once you get married, you should begin to pool." The husband and pastor adds.

"That is why the marriage vow says that you should not enter marriage indiscreetly." His wife adds, "You cannot say this is mine'. They get married but they have not come together."

It is not that we have never had problems," she insists, "but the important thing is to think it over and learn to say 'I am sorry, please forgive me. I will try to see it never happens again'. Then, take it to the Lord and pray together. These are some of the things that will let marriage stick. Say, 'I love you, I appreciate you, I thank you'. Your caring must be expressed."

The marriage counselor notes that secrets also cause marriages to fall apart. The disclosure clause in the marriage vows should be taken more seriously, she states. Dr. Douglas, as a community leader, is forced to make one admission.

**Challenge**

We cannot deny there is a different challenge today (compared to when they started). "It is challenging to live up to the Joneses. Try to be moderate. Live by principles. If not, you will drift." His wife gets the last word in. She concludes, "staying together has been a work of love. I love him for who he is, and he loves me for who I am. The love of God is shed abroad, but, in the natural, if you do not love each other, you will not stay together, her husband agrees. "There is a love which is beyond the ordinary. I have never doubted my wife. I have never thought that she would have another man with me. I would never betray her. She would never betray me."

The feeling is mutual." (Wilmot, 2001)

# MORE FROM ANDREW V. PUSEY

Anointing for Possibilities

The anointing of the Holy Spirit holds boundless potential. By harnessing this anointing, we are bestowed with the power to perform remarkable deeds that surpass our innate capabilities.

In the riveting "Anointing for Possibilities," the author adeptly unravels the immense power contained within the anointing for all believers and offers practical guidance on how to tap into this power to manifest extraordinary feats in your life and ministry.

As you delve into the pages of this book, anticipate a rejuvenating spiritual reawakening and a refreshing boost of energy poised to propel you toward your destined path! A world of limitless possibilities eagerly awaits your arrival!

# REFERENCES

Apple Podcasts. (2023, July 26). *The Naked Marriage with Dave & Ashley Willis on Apple Podcasts*. https://podcasts.apple.com/us/podcast/the-naked-marriage-with-dave-ashley-willis/id1437213097

*OFFICIAL KING JAMES BIBLE ONLINE*. (n.d.). https://www.kingjamesbibleonline.org/ [1]

Wilmot, C. (2001, November 4). An old-fashioned love. *https://jamaica-gleaner.com/*.

---

1. Note – Bible verses are quoted from the King James version of the Bible.

Made in the USA
Middletown, DE
15 October 2023